OXFORD STUDENT TEXTS

Series Editor: Steven Croft

Geoffrey Chaucer

The Merchant's Prologue and Tale

T0347133

Geoffrey Chaucer

The Merchant's Prologue and Tale

Edited by Steven Croft

OXFORD
UNIVERSITY PRESS

OXFORD
UNIVERSITY PRESS

Great Clarendon Street, Oxford OX2 6DP, United Kingdom

Oxford University Press is a department of the University of Oxford.
It furthers the University's objective of excellence in research, scholarship,
and education by publishing worldwide

Oxford is a registered trade mark of Oxford University Press
in the UK and in certain other countries

British Library Cataloguing in Publication Data

Data available

ISBN: 978-0-19-835538-0

12

Typeset by PDQ Digital Media Solutions, Bungay

Printed and bound by CPI Group (UK) Ltd, Croydon, CR0 4YY

Paper used in the production of this book is a natural, recyclable product made from
wood grown in sustainable forests. The manufacturing process conforms to the
environmental regulations of the country of origin.

The publishers would like to thank the following for permission to reproduce
photographs:

Pages 2, 7, 10, 107, 112: Mary Evans Picture Library; page 4: Westminster Abbey,
London, UK / Bridgeman Images; page 12: © Guildhall Art Gallery, City of London /
Bridgeman Images; page 93: Private Collection / © Look and Learn / Bridgeman Images;
page 100: Private Collection / Ken Welsh / Bridgeman Images; page 121: Mary Evans /
INTERFOTO / Bildarchiv Hansmann

Contents

Acknowledgements   vii

Foreword   ix

The Merchant's Tale in Context   1
Chaucer's life   1
Language in Chaucer's time   5
The literary context   5
Chaucer's works   6
The merchant class   8
Marriage   10

The Merchant's Tale   15
The Merchant's portrait: General Prologue   15
The Merchant's Prologue   16
The Merchant's Tale   17
Epilogue to the Merchant's Tale   52

Notes   53
The Merchant's portrait: General Prologue   53
The Merchant's Prologue: Lines 1–32   54
January and his desire to marry: Lines 33–54   55
In praise of marriage: Lines 55–98   56
The benefits of having a wife: Lines 99–180   58
The Merchant returns to his story: Lines 181–256   61
January receives advice: Lines 257–364   63
January chooses his wife: Lines 365–476   65
January is married: Lines 477–529   68
May gains an admirer: Lines 530–582   70
January takes May to bed: Lines 583–653   71
January sends May to Damyan: Lines 654–742   73
May is in love with Damyan: Lines 743–808   75
January is struck by blindness: Lines 809–919   77
May promises to be true, and Damyan hides in the tree:
    Lines 920–1006   80
Pluto and Proserpina intervene: Lines 1007–1107   81
May and Damyan make love: Lines 1108–1141   84

January's sight is restored: Lines 1142–1206   85
The Merchant's Epilogue   86

Interpretations   89
Narrative voice   89
Genre   90
Characterization   91
Themes   106
Language and style   114
Narrative techniques   120
The unity of Prologue and tale   122
Critical views   124

A Note on Chaucer's English   127

A Note on Pronunciation   135

Essay Questions   137

Chronology   139

Further Reading   141

Glossary   143

Acknowledgements

The publishers and editor would like to thank Professor Peter Mack for permission to adapt his sections entitled *A Note on Chaucer's English* and *A Note on Pronunciation* for this edition of *The Merchant's Tale*.

The text is taken from *The Riverside Chaucer*, Third Edition, edited by Larry D. Benson, copyright 1987 © by Houghton Mifflin Company.

Acknowledgements from Steven Croft

I would like to thank Sandra Haigh for her unstinting support in the production of this book. I am also grateful to Jan Doorly for her helpful and constructive advice and sensitive editing of the manuscript.

Editor

Steven Croft, the series editor, holds degrees from Leeds and Sheffield universities. He has taught at secondary and tertiary level and headed the Department of English and Humanities in a tertiary college. He has 25 years' examining experience at A level and is currently a Principal Examiner for English. He has written several books on teaching English at A level, and his publications for Oxford University Press include *Exploring Literature*, *Success in AQA Language and Literature* and *Exploring Language and Literature*.

Foreword

Oxford Student Texts have established a reputation for presenting literary texts to students in both a scholarly and an accessible way. The new editions aim to build on this successful approach. They have been written to help students, particularly those studying English literature for AS or A level, to develop an increased understanding of their texts. Each volume in the series, which covers a selection of key poetry and drama texts, consists of four main sections which link together to provide an integrated approach to the study of the text.

The first part provides important background information about the writer, his or her times and the factors that played an important part in shaping the work. This discussion sets the work in context and explores some key contextual factors.

This section is followed by the poetry or play itself. The text is presented without accompanying notes so that students can engage with it on their own terms without the influence of secondary ideas. To encourage this approach, the Notes are placed in the third section, immediately following the text. The Notes provide explanations of particular words, phrases, images, allusions and so forth, to help students gain a full understanding of the text. They also raise questions or highlight particular issues or ideas which are important to consider when arriving at interpretations.

The fourth section, Interpretations, goes on to discuss a range of issues in more detail. This involves an examination of the influence of contextual factors as well as looking at such aspects as language and style, and various critical views or interpretations. A range of activities for students to carry out, together with discussions as to how these might be approached, are integrated into this section.

At the end of each volume there is a selection of Essay Questions, a Chronology, and a Further Reading list.

We hope you enjoy reading this text and working with these supporting materials, and wish you every success in your studies.

Steven Croft   *Series Editor*

The Merchant's Tale in Context

Chaucer's life

There is much uncertainty surrounding Geoffrey Chaucer's exact date of birth, although it seems likely that he was born some time in the early 1340s (1343 is often given as the likely year) in London. The date of his death can be identified with more certainty. Records show that he died towards the end of 1400, the date of 25 October being accepted by many scholars.

Chaucer's father, John, was a prosperous London wine merchant. He had served in the military campaigns of 1327 and 1329, and was the deputy to the king's chief butler from 1347 to 1349. This gave him a minor connection with the court, and his wealth was increased through his inheritance of several properties. He died in 1366. Chaucer's mother also had inherited several properties, so the young Chaucer grew up in an affluent family with some links to the royal household.

There is little concrete evidence of the kind of education Chaucer received, and there is no record of whether he attended school. It is generally thought likely that he did, and he might have attended one of several prestigious schools in the area of London in which he lived. Equally, he could have been educated at home, either by his parents or private tutors.

Whatever form it took, it is certain that Chaucer received an education suitable to his social standing and one that provided him with the necessary skills for entry into a career of civil or court service. As part of his education, Chaucer would have learned Latin and would have gained some knowledge of Latin texts such as the writings of Virgil, Ovid and the fables of Aesop. French would also have been an important part of his education. In the fourteenth century, French was the language of the court and of all legal documents and proceedings; it was the standard language spoken by the middle and upper classes. It is clear that Chaucer was also familiar with Italian, and his writings reveal a knowledge of Italian authors of the period such as Dante, Petrarch and Boccaccio.

By 1357, Chaucer was a member of the court of Elizabeth, Countess of Ulster and wife of Lionel, the son of King Edward III. It is generally assumed that Chaucer was a page in Elizabeth's household, and as such he would have travelled around the country with her entourage. Pages were normally aged between 10 and 17 and performed a variety of functions including the duties of personal servants. They were not paid, and so needed the support of their families, but were given board, lodging and clothing by their employer. While in service, they were also educated in the manners and customs of upper-class society, and their position also gave them the opportunity to meet and possibly impress influential people who could advance their careers by giving them promotion or patronage.

Certainly employment in Elizabeth's household would have given Chaucer access to literature, both in written and oral form. Written

Chaucer, as depicted in an anonymous engraving

books were scarce as, before the invention of printing, they all had to be copied out by hand, and consequently only wealthy households possessed them. It was common for literature to be heard rather than read, with someone reading to a group of people gathered together. In Chaucer's time, the oral tradition in literature was still very strong.

In 1359, Chaucer became one of Prince Lionel's attendants and went to France on military service as a yeoman. He was captured in France in 1360 and ransomed for £16, which was a comparatively large sum. The king himself contributed to the ransom, and this suggests that he was considered of some value. He returned to France again in the autumn of 1360, carrying letters back to England from Lionel.

Little is known of Chaucer's life between 1360 and 1367, although we know that his father died in 1366. It seems that Chaucer was abroad again during part of this period and, towards the end of the 1360s, John of Gaunt became an important figure in his life. John of Gaunt was Duke of Lancaster and was, at that time, considered the wealthiest man in England. In 1369 Chaucer was once more on a military campaign in France with John of Gaunt. In 1372–1373 he was sent abroad to Genoa and Florence as part of important trade negotiations, possibly on behalf of the king.

On his return he was made, in 1374, the Controller of the Customs for wool, later adding skins and hides to his responsibilities. This was a very lucrative civil service appointment, but there are some indications that further promotions between 1377 and 1389 may have been blocked, possibly by enemies of the king. He was elected MP for Kent in 1386 but only remained in office a year, and he ceased to be Controller of Customs in 1386.

However, when Richard II – who had succeeded to the throne a decade before, at the age of ten – assumed real power in 1389, Chaucer seems to have regained favour and was given new jobs, one of which involved being responsible for the maintenance of the king's palaces. Later he was given the royal appointment of deputy forestership of North Petherton in Somerset. In 1399, Richard II was deposed by John of Gaunt's son, Henry Bolingbroke, who became Henry IV. Chaucer continued in favour under the new king and moved to a house in the garden of Westminster Abbey, where he lived until his death in October 1400. He was buried in Westminster Abbey.

King Richard II, in the 'Westminster Portrait' from the 1390s

Language in Chaucer's time

During Chaucer's life, three languages were important in English society:

- Latin – this was the language of the Church and of scholarship and learning. The ordinary people recognized those who used Latin as being educated and learned.
- French – in the early part of Chaucer's life this was the everyday language of the educated and cultured members of society. It was descended from the Norman French that was introduced after the conquest of England by William in 1066. This was the language of the royal court and of legal proceedings.
- English – this was the everyday language spoken by the people.

During Chaucer's time the importance of French as the language of the educated classes had begun to decline, and in 1362 Parliament was opened by a speech from the throne delivered in English for the first time. In the same year it became permissible for law court proceedings to be conducted in English.

The literary context

As time went on, more and more French works were translated into English, including philosophical and religious works. Other literature appeared in English, including ballads and romances. Romances were stories usually about love or adventure, involving characters from the upper end of society. These stories, such as *The Knight's Tale* in *The Canterbury Tales*, featured courtly and noble behaviour.

Fabliaux were also popular. These were bawdy tales about ordinary people, and usually involved sex and trickery of some kind, such as that seen in *The Miller's Tale*.

In addition to the works written in Latin already mentioned and works written in French such as the French romance, *Le Roman de la Rose*, Chaucer would also have been familiar with Italian literature.

Works such as Dante's *Divine Comedy*, Boccaccio's *Decameron* (a collection of tales about nobles escaping the Black Death), and the works of Petrarch all influenced Chaucer's writings in various ways.

Chaucer's works

One of the important features of Chaucer's work is that he drew on the French and Italian literature he knew well, both in terms of themes, ideas and stylistic and technical approaches, in order to create a new poetry in English which was entirely his own. The dating of some of Chaucer's works is not certain, but one of the most important of his early pieces was a translation of *Le Roman de la Rose*. His first major poem, *The Book of the Duchess*, which was written in 1369 or 1370, shows clearly the influence of French literature. The poem was written to commemorate the death of John of Gaunt's wife, Blanche, the Duchess of Lancaster. It is written as a dream-vision and is the first of four poems in which he wrote about dreams. It was followed by *The House of Fame*, *The Parliament of Fowls* and *The Legend of Good Women*.

Several of Chaucer's poems then began to show an Italian influence. One of them, the narrative poem *Troilus and Criseyde*, is considered by many to be his greatest single poem. It is about courtly love embodying the idea of idealized love, a theme he was to return to in *The Knight's Tale* in *The Canterbury Tales*.

The Canterbury Tales

Chaucer's greatest work, *The Canterbury Tales*, was written in the later years of his life, although it is possible that some parts of it had been written earlier. The poem centres on 29 pilgrims who meet by chance at the Tabard Inn in Southwark, London, before setting out on a pilgrimage to the shrine of Saint Thomas Becket at Canterbury. The pilgrims agree to tell each other tales on their journey to pass the time. Chaucer's original scheme was to have each of his pilgrims tell two tales on the way to Canterbury and two tales on the return trip to London. A prize of a free supper was to be given to the teller of the best story as judged by the Host, Harry Bailey.

As the pilgrims start their journey the tales begin. It is decided that the Knight, the highest in rank of the party, should tell the first tale. After several tales have been told the Clerk tells his tale of a young woman whose husband decides to test her loyalty through strange and extreme tests. At the end of that tale, the Merchant echoes the Clerk's closing words and expresses his feelings about his own less-than-happy experience of marriage. Hearing this, the Host asks the Merchant to tell them more about his views on marriage. The Merchant is reluctant to say more about his own marriage, but begins his tale about an old knight who marries a young and attractive woman.

Chaucer died before he was able to complete his ambitious scheme for *The Canterbury Tales*, which would have involved at least 116 stories. Before his death he had only written tales for 23 of the pilgrims, and even some of these are unfinished.

The Canterbury pilgrims on the road, as shown in the early fifteenth-century Ellesmere manuscript

Chaucer's overall scheme, therefore, is much more than simply a collection of stories. The setting within the context of a pilgrimage to Canterbury allows him to bring together a group of characters representing a whole cross-section of medieval society. The pilgrims are introduced in the *General Prologue*, and this is an important part of Chaucer's scheme, as he uses this introduction to give vivid portraits of each character in turn. They are drawn from all walks of life: the Knight and his son the Squire come from the ranks of the aristocracy; there are devout religious characters such as the Parson, the Prioress and the Nun, and others with rather more dubious morals such as the Pardoner and the Summoner, who use the power invested in them by the Church to exploit others and line their own pockets.

In addition, Chaucer introduces a variety of other pilgrims from all ranks of society, from the wealthy, middle-class Franklin to the rough-and-ready Miller and the lowly Ploughman. The various characters are also given a range of motivations for embarking on the pilgrimage. There are those whose motive is entirely spiritual, such as the Parson, and those who see it as an interesting and pleasurable outing, such as the Wife of Bath.

The merchant class

Chaucer would have been very familiar with the merchant class, as he had been brought up the son of a merchant. Although his father, John Chaucer, was not particularly prominent as a merchant he had gained some royal favour and had held the relatively important position of deputy to the royal butler, and in that role would have been closely involved in the wine trade. He had also held the position of collector of taxes at Southampton, and again that would have entailed close association with matters of business and finance.

Chaucer grew up a city with trade and commerce at its heart. But by the time he wrote *The Canterbury Tales* his own career had progressed beyond that of trade and he had become a highly respected courtier, well used to international travel, an effective civil servant and trusted employee of the Crown. However, he retained his detailed understanding of the world of the merchant.

In the fourteenth century, trade was an essential feature in the daily life of the bustling city. London merchants were at the heart of business and banking activities, which were often closely tied in to the world of politics. The position of merchants in society had developed well beyond that of simple traders, and they were firmly established as members of an increasingly wealthy and influential middle class. Some merchants had accrued great wealth, becoming richer than some of their aristocratic social superiors.

By the fourteenth century the merchant guilds had developed into powerful and influential organizations. In addition, the Merchant Adventurers – members of which were often based on the Continent – promoted the sale of English cloth in a wide variety of foreign cities, while the Merchants of the Staple oversaw the exportation of wool, the principal English export.

Chaucer's Merchant

Various aspects of the mercantile world of the fourteenth century are reflected in Chaucer's portrait of the Merchant in *The General Prologue*. However, the portrait has given rise to more than one interpretation. The first impression we get of the Merchant is of a well-dressed character, with his fashionable *forked berd* and expensive clothes, as he rides high on his horse; he has the air of a wealthy and successful man. He speaks, we are told, with dignity and seems to be a serious man of business. However, many critics have pointed to the line that follows this description:

Sownynge alwey th'encrees of his wynnyng.

This can suggest a slightly different image: someone who is always boasting about the profits he has made, and therefore a rather pompous character. The following lines mention his desire to make sure that the sea lanes are kept free from pirates, and this shows that his concern is to prevent anything from interfering with the profitable trade between England and the Continent. Despite the outward appearance of success, though, Chaucer reveals to us that the Merchant is actually in debt, although no one would have guessed.

Marriage

Several of *The Canterbury Tales* focus on the topic of marriage, and *The Merchant's Tale* forms a part of this sequence of tales. The debate is begun by the Wife of Bath in her tale, and is continued in *The Clerk's Tale*. The Merchant then contributes to this theme, and later both the Squire and the Franklin return to the topic.

The Church's view of marriage was that it was undesirable but necessary. The ideal state for everyone was to remain single and live a celibate life, as advocated by St Paul, St Jerome and the Greek philosopher Theophrastus, but the Church recognized that this was

The Merchant on his horse, in an illustration from the Ellesmere manuscript

not possible for all (and in fact, the human race would soon come to an end if everyone achieved it). Marriage was the acceptable alternative.

The status of women

The society of the Middle Ages was very much male dominated, and the status and rights of women were quite different from those of modern times.

- Both within the Church and in law, women had no legal or political power and were expected to be obedient (outwardly at least) to their fathers or husbands.
- Marriages were usually arranged, particularly among the aristocracy and middle-classes.
- Often the younger daughters of the wealthy were put into convents to train as nuns. They were usually sent to the convent at the age of 14.
- Women of lower status could earn their own living if they had some kind of skill or trade, such as the Wife of Bath, who earned money through weaving. In her case, though, she clearly obtained much of her wealth from marrying a string of elderly but wealthy husbands. Justinus, in advising January, warns him to think twice about giving away property or land when he marries. In the end, though, January offers to give May all he has if she remains true to him.
- The Church was one area in which a small number of women could achieve status and power in their own right. Those who became prioresses, in charge of the nunneries, became responsible for running large and lucrative estates and achieved some power and influence, becoming women of wealth and standing.
- When men were away fighting – in the crusades, for example – women ran their husbands' estates, and lower down the social order they took on tasks normally performed by men, such as brewing, leather working, baking and other trades.

Anti-feminism

In the Middle Ages the opinion that women were inferior to men in all respects, including intellectually, was strongly held by many. This view had several origins.

- Women were seen as symbolizing the temptations and evils of the flesh.
- The Church view was that women were the root cause of all human suffering and misery, based on the biblical account of Eve succumbing to the temptation that led to the Fall of Man and the banishment of Adam and Eve from the Garden of Eden.
- Over the centuries this idea had given rise to a wealth of anti-feminist writings of the kind that Justinus uses to try to persuade January to think again about what he is doing.
- Another source for anti-feminist ideas is the writings of the Greek philosopher Theophrastus, who depicts wives as being nagging, complaining and suspicious of their husbands.

A marble bust of Chaucer in the Guildhall Art Gallery, London

The Church's attitude towards women was necessarily ambiguous to some extent, however, as the Virgin Mary, the mother of Christ, was a woman. Mary was regarded as embodying all that was good and holy; she fulfilled the ideal of virginity and therefore was not corrupted by the sins of the flesh, yet was also a mother – the other role for which women could be respected.

In *The Merchant's Tale*, through the marriage of January and May, Chaucer focuses the audience's attention on all these issues and presents us with a variety of points of view on them. Clearly, January expresses his own views of marriage and women; contradictory though his comments often are, it is obvious to us what his beliefs and motivations are. Chaucer reveals May's attitude primarily through her actions, but her views are as clearly discernible as January's. In addition to the development of the central action of the plot, Chaucer broadens the debate further through the views of Placebo and Justinus and the heated argument between Pluto and Proserpina. These elements interlink and work together to create a tale that adds a further dimension to the debate on marriage that Chaucer had initiated in some of his other *Canterbury Tales*.

The Merchant's Tale

The Merchant's portrait: General Prologue

       A MARCHANT was ther with a forked berd,
271 In mottelee, and hye on horse he sat;
       Upon his heed a Flaundryssh bever hat,
       His bootes clasped faire and fetisly.
       His resons he spak ful solempnely,
275 Sownynge alwey th'encrees of his wynnyng.
       He wolde the see were kept for any thyng
       Bitwixe Middelburgh and Orewelle.
       Wel koude he in eschaunge sheeldes selle.
       This worthy man ful wel his wit bisette:
280 Ther wiste no wight that he was in dette,
       So estatly was he of his governaunce
       With his bargaynes and with his chevyssaunce.
       For sothe he was a worthy man with alle,
       But, sooth to seyn, I noot how men hym calle.

The Merchant's Prologue

The Prologe of the Marchantes Tale.

'Wepyng and waylyng, care and oother sorwe
I knowe ynogh, on even and a-morwe,'
Quod the Marchant, 'and so doon other mo
That wedded been. I trowe that it be so,
5   For wel I woot it fareth so with me.
I have a wyf, the worste that may be;
For thogh the feend to hire ycoupled were,
She wolde hym overmacche, I dar wel swere.
What sholde I yow reherce in special
10   Hir hye malice? She is a shrewe at al.
Ther is a long and large difference
Bitwix Grisildis grete pacience
And of my wyf the passyng crueltee.
Were I unbounden, also moot I thee,
15   I wolde nevere eft comen in the snare.
We wedded men lyven in sorwe and care.
Assaye whoso wole, and he shal fynde
That I seye sooth, by Seint Thomas of Ynde,
As for the moore part – I sey nat alle.
20   God shilde that it sholde so bifalle!
    'A, goode sire Hoost, I have ywedded bee
Thise monthes two, and moore nat, pardee;
And yet, I trowe, he that al his lyve
Wyflees hath been, though that men wolde him ryve
25   Unto the herte, ne koude in no manere
Tellen so muchel sorwe as I now heere
Koude tellen of my wyves cursednesse!'
    'Now,' quod oure Hoost, 'Marchaunt, so God
        yow blesse,
Syn ye so muchel knowen of that art

30 Ful hertely I pray yow telle us part.'
    'Gladly,' quod he, 'but of myn owene soore,
For soory herte, I telle may namoore.'

The Merchant's Tale

Heere bigynneth the Marchantes Tale.

    Whilom ther was dwellynge in Lumbardye
A worthy knyght, that born was of Pavye,
35 In which he lyved in greet prosperitee;
And sixty yeer a wyflees man was hee,
And folwed ay his bodily delyt
On wommen, ther as was his appetyt,
As doon thise fooles that been seculeer.
40 And whan that he was passed sixty yeer,
Were it for hoolynesse or for dotage
I kan nat seye, but swich a greet corage
Hadde this knyght to been a wedded man
That day and nyght he dooth al that he kan
45 T'espien where he myghte wedded be,
Preyinge oure Lord to graunten him that he
Mighte ones knowe of thilke blisful lyf
That is bitwixe an housbonde and his wyf,
And for to lyve under that hooly boond
50 With which that first God man and womman bond.
'Noon oother lyf,' seyde he, 'is worth a bene,
For wedlok is so esy and so clene,
That in this world it is a paradys.'
Thus seyde this olde knyght, that was so wys.
55   And certeinly, as sooth as God is kyng,
To take a wyf it is a glorious thyng,
And namely whan a man is oold and hoor;

Thanne is a wyf the fruyt of his tresor.
Thanne sholde he take a yong wyf and a feir,
60 On which he myghte engendren hym an heir,
And lede his lyf in joye and in solas,
Where as thise bacheleris synge 'allas,'
Whan that they fynden any adversitee
In love, which nys but childyssh vanytee.
65 And trewely it sit wel to be so,
That bacheleris have often peyne and wo;
On brotel ground they buylde, and brotelnesse
They fynde whan they wene sikernesse.
They lyve but as a bryd or as a beest,
70 In libertee and under noon arreest,
Ther as a wedded man in his estaat
Lyveth a lyf blisful and ordinaat
Under this yok of mariage ybounde.
Wel may his herte in joy and blisse habounde,
75 For who kan be so buxom as a wyf?
Who is so trewe, and eek so ententyf
To kepe hym, syk and hool, as is his make?
For wele or wo she wole hym nat forsake;
She nys nat wery hym to love and serve,
80 Though that he lye bedrede til he sterve.
And yet somme clerkes seyn it nys nat so,
Of whiche he Theofraste is oon of tho.
What force though Theofraste liste lye?
'Ne take no wyf,' quod he, 'for housbondrye,
85 As for to spare in houshold thy dispence.
A trewe servant dooth moore diligence
Thy good to kepe than thyn owene wyf,
For she wol clayme half part al hir lyf.
And if thou be syk, so God me save,
90 Thy verray freendes, or a trewe knave,
Wol kepe thee bet than she that waiteth ay

After thy good and hath doon many a day.
And if thou take a wyf unto thyn hoold
Ful lightly maystow been a cokewold.'
95   This sentence, and an hundred thynges worse,
Writeth this man, ther God his bones corse!
But take no kep of al swich vanytee;
Deffie Theofraste, and herke me.
        A wyf is Goddes yifte verraily;
100 Alle othere manere yiftes hardily,
As londes, rentes, pasture, or commune,
Or moebles – alle been yiftes of Fortune
That passen as a shadwe upon a wal.
But drede nat, if pleynly speke I shal:
105 A wyf wol laste, and in thyn hous endure,
Wel lenger than thee list, paraventure.
        Mariage is a ful greet sacrement.
He which that hath no wyf, I holde hym shent;
He lyveth helplees and al desolat –
110 I speke of folk in seculer estaat.
And herke why – I sey nat this for noght –
That womman is for mannes helpe ywroght.
The hye God, whan he hadde Adam maked,
And saugh him al allone, bely-naked,
115 God of his grete goodnesse seyde than,
'Lat us now make an helpe unto this man
Lyk to hymself'; and thanne he made him Eve.
Heere may ye se, and heerby may ye preve,
That wyf is mannes helpe and his confort,
120 His paradys terrestre, and his disport.
So buxom and so vertuous is she,
They moste nedes lyve in unitee.
O flessh they been, and o fleesh, as I gesse,
Hath but oon herte, in wele and in distresse.
125   A wyf! a, Seinte Marie, benedicite!

How myghte a man han any adversitee
That hath a wyf? Certes, I kan nat seye.
The blisse which that is bitwixe hem tweye
Ther may no tonge telle, or herte thynke.
130 If he be povre, she helpeth hym to swynke;
She kepeth his good, and wasteth never a deel;
Al that hire housbonde lust, hire liketh weel;
She seith nat ones 'nay,' whan he seith 'ye.'
'Do this,' seith he; 'Al redy, sire,' seith she.
135 O blisful ordre of wedlok precious,
Thou art so murye, and eek so vertuous,
And so commended and appreved eek
That every man that halt hym worth a leek
Upon his bare knees oughte al his lyf
140 Thanken his God that hym hath sent a wyf,
Or elles preye to God hym for to sende
A wyf to laste unto his lyves ende.
For thanne his lyf is set in sikernesse;
He may nat be deceyved, as I gesse,
145 So that he werke after his wyves reed.
Thanne may he boldely beren up his heed,
They been so trewe and therwithal so wyse;
For which, if thou wolt werken as the wyse,
Do alwey so as wommen wol thee rede.
150   Lo, how that Jacob, as thise clerkes rede,
By good conseil of his mooder Rebekke,
Boond the kydes skyn aboute his nekke,
For which his fadres benyson he wan.
        Lo Judith, as the storie eek telle kan,
155 By wys conseil she Goddes peple kepte,
And slow hym Olofernus, whil he slepte.
        Lo Abigayl, by good conseil how she
Saved hir housbonde Nabal whan that he
Sholde han be slayn; and looke, Ester also

160 By good conseil delyvered out of wo
The peple of God, and made hym Mardochee
Of Assuere enhaunced for to be.
    Ther nys no thyng in gree superlatyf,
As seith Senek, above an humble wyf.
165   Suffre thy wyves tonge, as Catoun bit;
She shal comande, and thou shalt suffren it,
And yet she wole obeye of curteisye.
A wyf is kepere of thyn housbondrye;
Wel may the sike man biwaille and wepe,
170 Ther as ther nys no wyf the hous to kepe.
I warne thee, if wisely thou wolt wirche,
Love wel thy wyf, as Crist loved his chirche.
If thou lovest thyself, thou lovest thy wyf;
No man hateth his flessh, but in his lyf
175 He fostreth it, and therfore bidde I thee
Cherisse thy wyf, or thou shalt nevere thee.
Housbonde and wyf, what so men jape or pleye,
Of worldly folk holden the siker weye;
They been so knyt ther may noon harm bityde,
180 And namely upon the wyves syde.
For which this Januarie, of whom I tolde,
Considered hath, inwith his dayes olde,
The lusty lyf, the vertuous quyete,
That is in mariage hony-sweete,
185 And for his freendes on a day he sente,
To tellen hem th'effect of his entente.
    With face sad his tale he hath hem toold.
He seyde, 'Freendes, I am hoor and oold,
And almoost, God woot, on my pittes brynke;
190 Upon my soule somwhat moste I thynke.
I have my body folily despended;
Blessed be God that it shal been amended!
For I wol be, certeyn, a wedded man,

And that anoon in al the haste I kan.
195 Unto som mayde fair and tendre of age,
     I prey yow, shapeth for my mariage
     Al sodeynly, for I wol nat abyde;
     And I wol fonde t'espien, on my syde,
     To whom I may be wedded hastily.
200 But forasmuche as ye been mo than I,
     Ye shullen rather swich a thyng espyen
     Than I, and where me best were to allyen.
          'But o thyng warne I yow, my freendes deere,
     I wol noon oold wyf han in no manere.
205 She shal nat passe twenty yeer, certayn;
     Oold fissh and yong flessh wolde I have fayn.
     Bet is,' quod he, 'a pyk than a pykerel,
     And bet than old boef is the tendre veel.
     I wol no womman thritty yeer of age;
210 It is but bene-straw and greet forage.
     And eek thise olde wydwes, God it woot,
     They konne so muchel craft on Wades boot.
     So muchel broken harm, whan that hem leste,
     That with hem sholde I nevere lyve in reste.
215 For sondry scoles maken sotile clerkis;
     Womman of manye scoles half a clerk is.
     But certeynly, a yong thyng may men gye,
     Right as men may warm wex with handes plye.
     Wherfore I sey yow pleynly, in a clause,
220 I wol noon oold wyf han right for this cause.
     For if so were I hadde swich myschaunce
     That I in hire ne koude han no plesaunce,
     Thanne sholde I lede my lyf in avoutrye
     And go streight to the devel whan I dye.
225 Ne children sholde I none upon hire geten;
     Yet were me levere houndes had me eten
     Than that myn heritage sholde falle

In straunge hand, and this I telle yow alle.
I dote nat; I woot the cause why
230 Men sholde wedde, and forthermoore woot I
Ther speketh many a man of mariage
That woot namoore of it than woot my page
For whiche causes man sholde take a wyf.
If he ne may nat lyven chaast his lyf,
235 Take hym a wyf with greet devocioun,
By cause of leveful procreacioun
Of children to th'onour of God above,
And nat oonly for paramour or love;
And for they sholde leccherye eschue,
240 And yelde hir dette whan that it is due;
Or for that ech of hem sholde helpen oother
In meschief, as a suster shal the brother,
And lyve in chastitee ful holily.
But sires, by youre leve, that am nat I.
245 For – God be thanked! – I dar make avaunt
I feele my lymes stark and suffisaunt
To do al that a man bilongeth to;
I woot myselven best what I may do.
Though I be hoor, I fare as dooth a tree
250 That blosmeth er that fruyt ywoxen bee;
And blosmy tree nys neither drye ne deed.
I feele me nowhere hoor but on myn heed;
Myn herte and alle my lymes been as grene
As laurer thurgh the yeer is for to sene.
255 And syn that ye han herd al myn entente,
I prey yow to my wyl ye wole assente.'
    Diverse men diversely hym tolde
Of mariage manye ensamples olde.
Somme blamed it, somme preysed it, certeyn,
260 But atte laste, shortly for to seyn,
As al day falleth altercacioun

23

Bitwixen freendes in disputisoun,
Ther fil a stryf bitwixe his bretheren two,
Of whiche that oon was cleped Placebo;
265 Justinus soothly called was that oother.
    Placebo seyde, 'O Januarie, brother,
Ful litel nede hadde ye, my lord so deere,
Conseil to axe of any that is heere,
But that ye been so ful of sapience
270 That yow ne liketh, for youre heighe prudence,
To weyven fro the word of Salomon.
This word seyde he unto us everychon:
"Wirk alle thyng by conseil," thus seyde he,
"And thanne shaltow nat repente thee."
275 But though that Salomon spak swich a word,
Myn owene deere brother and my lord,
So wysly God my soule brynge at reste,
I holde youre owene conseil is the beste.
For, brother myn, of me taak this motyf:
280 I have now been a court-man al my lyf,
And God it woot, though I unworthy be,
I have stonden in ful greet degree
Abouten lordes of ful heigh estaat;
Yet hadde I nevere with noon of hem debaat.
285 I nevere hem contraried, trewely;
I woot wel that my lord kan moore than I.
With that he seith, I holde it ferme and stable;
I seye the same, or elles thyng semblable.
A ful greet fool is any conseillour
290 That serveth any lord of heigh honour,
That dar presume, or elles thenken it,
That his conseil sholde passe his lordes wit.
Nay, lordes been no fooles, by my fay!
Ye han youreselven shewed heer to-day
295 So heigh sentence, so holily and weel,

That I consente and conferme everydeel
Youre wordes alle and youre opinioun.
By God, ther nys no man in al this toun,
Ne in Ytaille, that koude bet han sayd!
300 Crist halt hym of this conseil ful wel apayd.
And trewely, it is an heigh corage
Of any man that stapen is in age
To take a yong wyf; by my fader kyn,
Youre herte hangeth on a joly pyn!
305 Dooth now in this matiere right as yow leste,
For finally I holde it for the beste.'
    Justinus, that ay stille sat and herde,
Right in this wise he to Placebo answerde:
'Now, brother myn, be pacient, I preye,
310 Syn ye han seyd, and herkneth what I seye.
Senek, amonges othere wordes wyse,
Seith that a man oghte hym right wel avyse
To whom he yeveth his lond or his catel.
And syn I oghte avyse me right wel
315 To whom I yeve my good awey fro me,
Wel muchel moore I oghte avysed be
To whom I yeve my body for alwey.
I warne yow wel, it is no childes pley
To take a wyf withouten avysement.
320 Men moste enquere – this is myn assent –
Wher she be wys, or sobre, or dronkelewe,
Or proud, or elles ootherweys a shrewe,
A chidestere, or wastour of thy good,
Or riche, or poore, or elles mannyssh wood.
325 Al be it so that no man fynden shal
Noon in this world that trotteth hool in al,
Ne man, ne beest, swich as men koude devyse;
But nathelees it oghte ynough suffise
With any wyf, if so were that she hadde

330 Mo goode thewes than hire vices badde;
     And al this axeth leyser for t'enquere.
     For, God it woot, I have wept many a teere
     Ful pryvely, syn I have had a wyf.
     Preyse whoso wole a wedded mannes lyf,
335 Certein I fynde in it but cost and care
     And observances, of alle blisses bare.
     And yet, God woot, my neighebores aboute,
     And namely of wommen many a route,
     Seyn that I have the mooste stedefast wyf,
340 And eek the mekeste oon that bereth lyf;
     But I woot best where wryngeth me my sho.
     Ye mowe, for me, right as yow liketh do;
     Avyseth yow – ye been a man of age –
     How that ye entren into mariage,
345 And namely with a yong wyf and a fair.
     By hym that made water, erthe, and air,
     The yongeste man that is in al this route
     Is bisy ynough to bryngen it aboute
     To han his wyf allone. Trusteth me,
350 Ye shul nat plesen hire fully yeres thre –
     This is to seyn, to doon hire ful plesaunce.
     A wyf axeth ful many an observaunce.
     I prey yow that ye be nat yvele apayd.'
        'Wel,' quod this Januarie, 'and hastow ysayd?
355 Straw for thy Senek, and for thy proverbes!
     I counte nat a panyer ful of herbes
     Of scole-termes. Wyser men than thow,
     As thou hast herd, assenteden right now
     To my purpos. Placebo, what sey ye?'
360   'I seye it is a cursed man,' quod he,
     'That letteth matrimoigne, sikerly.'
     And with that word they rysen sodeynly,
     And been assented fully that he sholde

Be wedded whanne hym liste and where he wolde.
365   Heigh fantasye and curious bisynesse
Fro day to day gan in the soule impresse
Of Januarie aboute his mariage.
Many fair shap and many a fair visage
Ther passeth thurgh his herte nyght by nyght,
370 As whoso tooke a mirour, polisshed bryght,
And sette it in a commune market-place,
Thanne sholde he se ful many a figure pace
By his mirour; and in the same wyse
Gan Januarie inwith his thoght devyse
375 Of maydens whiche that dwelten hym bisyde.
He wiste nat wher that he myghte abyde.
For if that oon have beaute in hir face,
Another stant so in the peples grace
For hire sadnesse and hire benyngnytee
380 That of the peple grettest voys hath she;
And somme were riche and hadden badde name.
But nathelees, bitwixe ernest and game,
He atte laste apoynted hym on oon,
And leet alle othere from his herte goon,
385 And chees hire of his owene auctoritee;
For love is blynd alday, and may nat see.
And whan that he was in his bed ybroght,
He purtreyed in his herte and in his thoght
Hir fresshe beautee and hir age tendre,
390 Hir myddel smal, hire armes longe and sklendre,
Hir wise governaunce, hir gentillesse,
Hir wommanly berynge, and hire sadnesse.
And whan that he on hire was condescended,
Hym thoughte his choys myghte nat ben amended.
395 For whan that he hymself concluded hadde,
Hym thoughte ech oother mannes wit so badde

That inpossible it were to repplye
Agayn his choys; this was his fantasye.
His freendes sente he to, at his instaunce,
400 And preyed hem to doon hym that plesaunce,
That hastily they wolden to hym come;
He wolde abregge hir labour, alle and some.
Nedeth namoore for hym to go ne ryde;
He was apoynted ther he wolde abyde.
405   Placebo cam, and eek his freendes soone,
And alderfirst he bad hem alle a boone,
That noon of hem none argumentes make
Agayn the purpos which that he hath take,
Which purpos was plesant to God, seyde he,
410 And verray ground of his prosperitee.
        He seyde ther was a mayden in the toun,
Which that of beautee hadde greet renoun,
Al were it so she were of smal degree;
Suffiseth hym hir yowthe and hir beautee.
415 Which mayde, he seyde, he wolde han to his wyf,
To lede in ese and hoolynesse his lyf;
And thanked God that he myghte han hire al,
That no wight his blisse parten shal.
And preyed hem to laboure in this nede,
420 And shapen that he faille nat to spede;
For thanne, he seyde, his spirit was at ese.
'Thanne is,' quod he, 'no thyng may me displese,
Save o thyng priketh in my conscience,
The which I wol reherce in youre presence.
425   'I have,' quod he, 'herd seyd, ful yoore ago,
Ther may no man han parfite blisses two –
This is to seye, in erthe and eek in hevene.
For though he kepe hym fro the synnes sevene,
And eek from every branche of thilke tree,
430 Yet is ther so parfit felicitee

And so greet ese and lust in mariage
That evere I am agast now in myn age
That I shal lede now so myrie a lyf,
So delicat, withouten wo and stryf,
435 That I shal have myn hevene in erthe heere.
For sith that verray hevene is boght so deere
With tribulacion and greet penaunce,
How sholde I thanne, that lyve in swich plesaunce
As alle wedded men doon with hire wyvys,
440 Come to the blisse ther Crist eterne on lyve ys?
This is my drede, and ye, my bretheren tweye,
Assoilleth me this question, I preye.'
   Justinus, which that hated his folye,
Answerde anon right in his japerye;
445 And for he wolde his longe tale abregge,
He wolde noon auctoritee allegge,
But seyde, 'Sire, so ther be noon obstacle
Oother than this, God of his hygh myracle
And of his mercy may so for yow wirche
450 That, er ye have youre right of hooly chirche,
Ye may repente of wedded mannes lyf,
In which ye seyn ther is no wo ne stryf.
And elles, God forbede but he sente
A wedded man hym grace to repente
455 Wel ofte rather than a sengle man!
And therfore, sire – the beste reed I kan –
Dispeire yow noght, but have in youre memorie,
Paraunter she may be youre purgatorie!
She may be Goddes meene and Goddes whippe;
460 Thanne shal youre soule up to hevene skippe
Swifter than dooth an arwe out of a bowe.
I hope to God, herafter shul ye knowe
That ther nys no so greet felicitee
In mariage, ne nevere mo shal bee,

465 That yow shal lette of youre savacion,
     So that ye use, as skile is and reson,
     The lustes of youre wyf attemprely,
     And that ye plese hire nat to amorously,
     And that ye kepe yow eek from oother synne.
470 My tale is doon, for my wit is thynne.
     Beth nat agast herof, my brother deere,
     But lat us waden out of this mateere.
     The Wyf of Bathe, if ye han understonde,
     Of mariage, which we have on honde,
475 Declared hath ful wel in litel space.
     Fareth now wel. God have yow in his grace.'
         And with this word this Justyn and his brother
     Han take hir leve, and ech of hem of oother.
     For whan they saughe that it moste nedes be,
480 They wroghten so, by sly and wys tretee,
     That she, this mayden which that Mayus highte,
     As hastily as evere that she myghte
     Shal wedded be unto this Januarie.
     I trowe it were to longe yow to tarie,
485 If I yow tolde of every scrit and bond
     By which that she was feffed in his lond,
     Or for to herknen of hir riche array.
     But finally ycomen is the day
     That to the chirche bothe be they went
490 For to receyve the hooly sacrement.
     Forth comth the preest, with stole aboute his nekke,
     And bad hire be lyk Sarra and Rebekke
     In wysdom and in trouthe of mariage;
     And seyde his orisons, as is usage,
495 And croucheth hem, and bad God sholde hem
         blesse,
     And made al siker ynogh with hoolynesse.
         Thus been they wedded with solempnitee,

And at the feeste sitteth he and she
With othere worthy folk upon the deys.
500   Al ful of joye and blisse is the paleys,
And ful of instrumentz and of vitaille,
The mooste deyntevous of al Ytaille.
Biforn hem stoode instrumentz of swich soun
That Orpheus, ne of Thebes Amphioun,
505   Ne maden nevere swich a melodye.
At every cours thanne cam loud mynstralcye
That nevere tromped Joab for to heere,
Nor he Theodomas, yet half so cleere
At Thebes whan the citee was in doute.
510   Bacus the wyn hem shynketh al aboute,
And Venus laugheth upon every wight,
For Januarie was bicome hir knyght
And wolde bothe assayen his corage
In libertee, and eek in mariage;
515   And with hire fyrbrond in hire hand aboute
Daunceth biforn the bryde and al the route.
And certeinly, I dar right wel seyn this,
Ymeneus, that god of weddyng is,
Saugh nevere his lyf so myrie a wedded man.
520   Hoold thou thy pees, thou poete Marcian,
That writest us that ilke weddyng murie
Of hire Philologie and hym Mercurie,
And of the songes that the Muses songe!
To smal is bothe thy penne, and eek thy tonge,
525   For to descryven of this mariage.
Whan tendre youthe hath wedded stoupyng age,
Ther is swich myrthe that it may nat be writen.
Assayeth it yourself; thanne may ye witen
If that I lye or noon in this matiere.
530   Mayus, that sit with so benyngne a chiere,
Hire to biholde it semed fayerye.

Queene Ester looked nevere with swich an ye
On Assuer, so meke a look hath she.
I may yow nat devyse al hir beautee.
535 But thus muche of hire beautee telle I may,
That she was lyk the brighte morwe of May,
Fulfild of alle beautee and plesaunce.
    This Januarie is ravysshed in a traunce
At every tyme he looked on hir face;
540 But in his herte he gan hire to manace
That he that nyght in armes wolde hire streyne
Harder than evere Parys dide Eleyne.
But nathelees yet hadde he greet pitee
That thilke nyght offenden hire moste he,
545 And thoughte, 'Allas! O tendre creature,
Now wolde God ye myghte wel endure
Al my corage, it is so sharp and keene!
I am agast ye shul it nat susteene.
But God forbede that I dide al my myght!
550 Now wolde God that it were woxen nyght,
And that the nyght wolde lasten everemo.
I wolde that al this peple were ago.'
And finally he dooth al his labour,
As he best myghte, savynge his honour,
555 To haste hem fro the mete in subtil wyse.
    The tyme cam that resoun was to ryse;
And after that men daunce and drynken faste,
And spices al aboute the hous they caste,
And ful of joye and blisse is every man –
560 Al but a squyer, highte Damyan,
Which carf biforn the knyght ful many a day.
He was so ravysshed on his lady May
That for the verray peyne he was ny wood.
Almoost he swelte and swowned ther he stood,
565 So soore hath Venus hurt hym with hire brond,

As that she bar it daunsynge in hire hond;
And to his bed he wente hym hastily.
Namoore of hym at this tyme speke I,
But there I lete hym wepe ynogh and pleyne
570 Til fresshe May wol rewen on his peyne.
    O perilous fyr, that in the bedstraw bredeth!
O famulier foo, that his servyce bedeth!
O servant traytour, false hoomly hewe,
Lyk to the naddre in bosom sly untrewe,
575 God shilde us alle from youre aqueyntaunce!
O Januarie, dronken in plesaunce
In mariage, se how thy Damyan,
Thyn owene squier and thy borne man,
Entendeth for to do thee vileynye.
580 God graunte thee thyn hoomly fo t'espye!
For in this world nys worse pestilence
Than hoomly foo al day in thy presence.
Parfourned hath the sonne his ark diurne;
No lenger may the body of hym sojurne
585 On th'orisonte, as in that latitude.
Night with his mantel, that is derk and rude,
Gan oversprede the hemysperie aboute;
For which departed is this lusty route
Fro Januarie, with thank on every syde.
590 Hoom to hir houses lustily they ryde,
Where as they doon hir thynges as hem leste,
And whan they sye hir tyme, goon to reste.
Soone after that, this hastif Januarie
Wolde go to bedde; he wolde no lenger tarye.
595 He drynketh ypocras, clarree, and vernage
Of spices hoote t'encreessen his corage;
And many a letuarie hath he ful fyn,
Swiche as the cursed monk, daun Constantyn,
Hath writen in his book *De Coitu*;

600   To eten hem alle he nas no thyng eschu.
       And to his privee freendes thus seyde he:
       'For Goddes love, as soone as it may be,
       Lat voyden al this hous in curteys wyse.'
       And they han doon right as he wol devyse.
605   Men drynken and the travers drawe anon.
       The bryde was broght abedde as stille as stoon;
       And whan the bed was with the preest yblessed,
       Out of the chambre hath every wight hym dressed;
       And Januarie hath faste in armes take
610   His fresshe May, his paradys, his make.
       He lulleth hire; he kisseth hire ful ofte;
       With thikke brustles of his berd unsofte,
       Lyk to the skyn of houndfyssh, sharp as brere –
       For he was shave al newe in his manere –
615   He rubbeth hire aboute hir tendre face,
       And seyde thus, 'Allas! I moot trespace
       To yow, my spouse, and yow greetly offende
       Er tyme come that I wil doun descende.
       But nathelees, considereth this,' quod he,
620   'Ther nys no werkman, whatsoevere he be,
       That may bothe werke wel and hastily;
       This wol be doon at leyser parfitly.
       It is no fors how longe that we pleye;
       In trewe wedlok coupled be we tweye,
625   And blessed be the yok that we been inne,
       For in oure actes we mowe do no synne.
       A man may do no synne with his wyf,
       Ne hurte hymselven with his owene knyf,
       For we han leve to pleye us by the lawe.'
630   Thus laboureth he til that the day gan dawe;
       And thanne he taketh a sop in fyn clarree,
       And upright in his bed thanne sitteth he,
       And after that he sang ful loude and cleere,

And kiste his wyf, and made wantown cheere.
635 He was al coltissh, ful of ragerye,
And ful of jargon as a flekked pye.
The slakke skyn aboute his nekke shaketh
Whil that he sang, so chaunteth he and craketh.
But God woot what that May thoughte in hir herte,
640 Whan she hym saugh up sittynge in his sherte,
In his nyght-cappe, and with his nekke lene;
She preyseth nat his pleyyng worth a bene.
Thanne seide he thus, 'My reste wol I take;
Now day is come, I may no lenger wake.'
645 And doun he leyde his heed and sleep til pryme.
And afterward, whan that he saugh his tyme,
Up ryseth Januarie; but fresshe May
Heeld hire chambre unto the fourthe day,
As usage is of wyves for the beste.
650 For every labour somtyme moot han reste,
Or elles longe may he nat endure;
This is to seyn, no lyves creature,
Be it of fyssh, or bryd, or beest, or man.
    Now wol I speke of woful Damyan,
655 That langwissheth for love, as ye shul heere;
Therfore I speke to hym in this manere:
I seye, 'O sely Damyan, allas!
Andswere to my demaunde, as in this cas.
How shaltow to thy lady, fresshe May,
660 Telle thy wo? She wole alwey seye nay.
Eek if thou speke, she wol thy wo biwreye.
God be thyn helpe! I kan no bettre seye.'
    This sike Damyan in Venus fyr
So brenneth that he dyeth for desyr,
665 For which he putte his lyf in aventure.
No lenger myghte he in this wise endure,
But prively a penner gan he borwe,

And in a lettre wroot he al his sorwe,
In manere of a compleynt or a lay,
670   Unto his faire, fresshe lady May;
And in a purs of sylk heng on his sherte
He hath it put, and leyde it at his herte.
    The moone, that at noon was thilke day
That Januarie hath wedded fresshe May
675   In two of Tawr, was into Cancre glyden;
So longe hath Mayus in hir chambre abyden,
As custume is unto thise nobles alle.
A bryde shal nat eten in the halle
Til dayes foure, or thre dayes atte leeste,
680   Ypassed been; thanne lat hire go to feeste.
The fourthe day compleet fro noon to noon,
Whan that the heighe masse was ydoon,
In halle sit this Januarie and May,
As fressh as is the brighte someres day.
685   And so bifel how that this goode man
Remembred hym upon this Damyan,
And seyde, 'Seynte Marie! how may this be,
That Damyan entendeth nat to me?
Is he ay syk, or how may this bityde?'
690   His squieres, whiche that stooden ther bisyde,
Excused hym by cause of his siknesse,
Which letted hym to doon his bisynesse;
Noon oother cause myghte make hym tarye.
    'That me forthynketh,' quod this Januarie,
695   'He is a gentil squier, by my trouthe!
If that he deyde, it were harm and routhe.
He is as wys, discreet, and as secree
As any man I woot of his degree,
And therto manly, and eek servysable,
700   And for to been a thrifty man right able.
But after mete, as soone as evere I may,

I wol myself visite hym, and eek May,
To doon hym al the confort that I kan.'
And for that word hym blessed every man,
705 That of his bountee and his gentillesse
He wolde so conforten in siknesse
His squier, for it was a gentil dede.
'Dame,' quod this Januarie, 'taak good hede,
At after-mete ye with youre wommen alle,
710 Whan ye han been in chambre out of this halle,
That alle ye go se this Damyan.
Dooth hym disport – he is a gentil man;
And telleth hym that I wol hym visite,
Have I no thyng but rested me a lite;
715 And spede yow faste, for I wole abyde
Til that ye slepe faste by my syde.'
And with that word he gan to hym to calle
A squier, that was marchal of his halle,
And tolde hym certeyn thynges, what he wolde.
720   This fresshe May hath streight hir wey yholde
With alle hir wommen unto Damyan.
Doun by his beddes syde sit she than,
Confortynge hym as goodly as she may.
This Damyan, whan that his tyme he say,
725 In secree wise his purs and eek his bille,
In which that he ywriten hadde his wille,
Hath put into hire hand, withouten moore,
Save that he siketh wonder depe and soore,
And softely to hire right thus seyde he:
730 'Mercy! And that ye nat discovere me,
For I am deed if that this thyng be kyd.'
This purs hath she inwith hir bosom hyd
And wente hire wey; ye gete namoore of me.
But unto Januarie ycomen is she,
735 That on his beddes syde sit ful softe.

He taketh hire, and kisseth hire ful ofte,
And leyde hym doun to slepe, and that anon.
She feyned hire as that she moste gon
Ther as ye woot that every wight moot neede;
740 And whan she of this bille hath taken heede,
She rente it al to cloutes atte laste,
And in the pryvee softely it caste.
    Who studieth now but faire fresshe May?
Adoun by olde Januarie she lay,
745 That sleep til that the coughe hath hym awaked.
Anon he preyde hire strepen hire al naked;
He wolde of hire, he seyde, han som plesaunce;
He seyde hir clothes dide hym encombraunce,
And she obeyeth, be hire lief or looth.
750 But lest that precious folk be with me wrooth,
How that he wroghte, I dar nat to yow telle,
Or wheither hire thoughte it paradys or helle.
But heere I lete hem werken in hir wyse
Til evensong rong and that they moste aryse.
755   Were it by destynee or by aventure,
Were it by influence or by nature,
Or constellacion, that in swich estaat
The hevene stood that tyme fortunaat
Was for to putte a bille of Venus werkes –
760 For alle thyng hath tyme, as seyn thise clerkes –
To any womman for to gete hire love,
I kan nat seye; but grete God above,
That knoweth that noon act is causelees,
He deme of al, for I wole holde my pees.
765 But sooth is this, how that this fresshe May
Hath take swich impression that day
Of pitee of this sike Damyan
That from hire herte she ne dryve kan
The remembrance for to doon hym ese.

770 'Certeyn,' thoghte she, 'whom that this thyng
        displese
    I rekke noght, for heere I hym assure
    To love hym best of any creature,
    Though he namoore hadde than his sherte.'
    Lo, pitee renneth soone in gentil herte!
775   Heere may ye se how excellent franchise
    In wommen is, whan they hem narwe avyse.
    Som tyrant is, as ther be many oon
    That hath an herte as hard as any stoon,
    Which wolde han lat hym sterven in the place
780 Wel rather than han graunted hym hire grace,
    And hem rejoysen in hire crueel pryde,
    And rekke nat to been an homycide.
      This gentil May, fulfilled of pitee,
    Right of hire hand a lettre made she,
785 In which she graunteth hym hire verray grace.
    Ther lakketh noght oonly but day and place
    Wher that she myghte unto his lust suffise,
    For it shal be right as he wole devyse.
    And whan she saugh hir tyme, upon a day
790 To visite this Damyan gooth May,
    And sotilly this lettre doun she threste
    Under his pilwe; rede it if hym leste.
    She taketh hym by the hand and harde hym twiste
    So secrely that no wight of it wiste,
795 And bad hym been al hool, and forth she wente
    To Januarie, whan that he for hire sente.
      Up riseth Damyan the nexte morwe;
    Al passed was his siknesse and his sorwe.
    He kembeth hym, he preyneth hym and pyketh,
800 He dooth al that his lady lust and lyketh,
    And eek to Januarie he gooth as lowe
    As evere dide a dogge for the bowe.

He is so plesant unto every man
(For craft is al, whoso that do it kan)
805 That every wight is fayn to speke hym good,
And fully in his lady grace he stood.
Thus lete I Damyan aboute his nede,
And in my tale forth I wol procede.
 Somme clerkes holden that felicitee
810 Stant in delit, and therfore certeyn he,
This noble Januarie, with al his myght,
In honest wyse, as longeth to a knyght,
Shoop hym to lyve ful deliciously.
His housynge, his array, as honestly
815 To his degree was maked as a kynges.
Amonges othere of his honeste thynges,
He made a gardyn, walled al with stoon;
So fair a gardyn woot I nowher noon.
For, out of doute, I verraily suppose
820 That he that wroot the Romance of the Rose
Ne koude of it the beautee wel devyse;
Ne Priapus ne myghte nat suffise,
Though he be god of gardyns, for to telle
The beautee of the gardyn and the welle
825 That stood under a laurer alwey grene.
Ful ofte tyme he Pluto and his queene,
Proserpina, and al hire fayerye,
Disporten hem and maken melodye
Aboute that welle, and daunced, as men tolde.
830 This noble knyght, this Januarie the olde,
Swich deyntee hath in it to walke and pleye,
That he wol no wight suffren bere the keye
Save he hymself; for of the smale wyket
He baar alwey of silver a clyket,
835 With which, whan that hym leste, he it unshette.
And whan he wolde paye his wyf hir dette

In somer seson, thider wolde he go,
And May his wyf, and no wight but they two;
And thynges whiche that were nat doon abedde,
840 He in the gardyn parfourned hem and spedde.
And in this wyse, many a murye day,
Lyved this Januarie and fresshe May.
But worldly joye may nat alwey dure
To Januarie, ne to no creature.
845   O sodeyn hap! O thou Fortune unstable!
Lyk to the scorpion so deceyvable,
That flaterest with thyn heed whan thou wolt stynge;
Thy tayl is deeth, thurgh thyn envenymynge.
O brotil joye! O sweete venym queynte!
850 O monstre, that so subtilly kanst peynte
Thy yiftes under hewe of stidefastnesse,
That thou deceyvest bothe moore and lesse!
Why hastow Januarie thus deceyved,
That haddest hym for thy fulle freend receyved?
855 And now thou hast biraft hym bothe his yen,
For sorwe of which desireth he to dyen.
    Allas, this noble Januarie free,
Amydde his lust and his prosperitee,
Is woxen blynd, and that al sodeynly.
860 He wepeth and he wayleth pitously;
And therwithal the fyr of jalousie,
Lest that his wyf sholde falle in som folye,
So brente his herte that he wolde fayn
That som man bothe hire and hym had slayn.
865 For neither after his deeth nor in his lyf
Ne wolde he that she were love ne wyf,
But evere lyve as wydwe in clothes blake,
Soul as the turtle that lost hath hire make.
But atte laste, after a month or tweye,
870 His sorwe gan aswage, sooth to seye;

For whan he wiste it may noon oother be,
He paciently took his adversitee,
Save, out of doute, he may nat forgoon
That he nas jalous everemoore in oon;

875 Which jalousye it was so outrageous
That neither in halle, n'yn noon oother hous,
Ne in noon oother place, neverthemo,
He nolde suffre hire for to ryde or go,
But if that he had hond on hire alway;

880 For which ful ofte wepeth fresshe May,
That loveth Damyan so benyngnely
That she moot outher dyen sodeynly,
Or elles she moot han hym as hir leste.
She wayteth whan hir herte wolde breste.

885   Upon that oother syde Damyan
Bicomen is the sorwefulleste man
That evere was, for neither nyght ne day
Ne myghte he speke a word to fresshe May,
As to his purpos, of no swich mateere,

890 But if that Januarie moste it heere,
That hadde an hand upon hire everemo.
But nathelees, by writyng to and fro
And privee signes wiste he what she mente,
And she knew eek the fyn of his entente.

895   O Januarie, what myghte it thee availle,
Thogh thou myghtest se as fer as shippes saille?
For as good is blynd deceyved be
As to be deceyved whan a man may se.
     Lo, Argus, which that hadde an hondred yen,

900 For al that evere he koude poure or pryen,
Yet was he blent, and, God woot, so been mo
That wenen wisly that it be nat so.
Passe over is an ese, I sey namoore.
     This fresshe May, that I spak of so yoore,

905 In warm wex hath emprented the clyket
That Januarie bar of the smale wyket,
By which into his gardyn ofte he wente;
And Damyan, that knew al hire entente,
The cliket countrefeted pryvely.
910 Ther nys namoore to seye, but hastily
Som wonder by this clyket shal bityde,
Which ye shul heeren, if ye wole abyde.
    O noble Ovyde, ful sooth seystou, God woot,
What sleighte is it, thogh it be long and hoot,
915 That Love nyl fynde it out in som manere?
By Piramus and Tesbee may men leere;
Thogh they were kept ful longe streite overal,
They been accorded, rownynge thurgh a wal,
Ther no wight koude han founde out swich a
        sleighte.
920   But now to purpos: er that dayes eighte
Were passed [of] the month of [Juyn], bifil
That Januarie hath caught so greet a wil,
Thurgh eggyng of his wyf, hym for to pleye
In his gardyn, and no wight but they tweye,
925 That in a morwe unto his May seith he:
'Rys up, my wyf, my love, my lady free!
The turtles voys is herd, my dowve sweete;
The wynter is goon with alle his reynes weete.
Com forth now, with thyne eyen columbyn!
930 How fairer been thy brestes than is wyn!
The gardyn is enclosed al aboute;
Com forth, my white spouse! Out of doute
Thou hast me wounded in myn herte, O wyf!
No spot of thee ne knew I al my lyf.
935 Com forth, and lat us taken oure disport;
I chees thee for my wyf and my confort.'
    Swiche olde lewed wordes used he.

On Damyan a signe made she,
That he sholde go biforn with his cliket.
940 This Damyan thanne hath opened the wyket,
And in he stirte, and that in swich manere
That no wight myghte it se neither yheere,
And stille he sit under a bussh anon.
    This Januarie, as blynd as is a stoon,
945 With Mayus in his hand, and no wight mo,
Into his fresshe gardyn is ago,
And clapte to the wyket sodeynly.
    'Now wyf,' quod he, 'heere nys but thou and I,
That art the creature that I best love.
950 For by that Lord that sit in hevene above,
Levere ich hadde to dyen on a knyf
Than thee offende, trewe deere wyf!
For Goddes sake, thenk how I thee chees,
Noght for no coveitise, doutelees,
955 But oonly for the love I had to thee.
And though that I be oold and may nat see,
Beth to me trewe, and I wol telle yow why.
Thre thynges, certes, shal ye wynne therby:
First, love of Crist, and to yourself honour,
960 And al myn heritage, toun and tour;
I yeve it yow, maketh chartres as yow leste;
This shal be doon to-morwe er sonne reste,
So wisly God my soule brynge in blisse.
I prey yow first, in covenant ye me kisse;
965 And though that I be jalous, wyte me noght.
Ye been so depe enprented in my thoght
That, whan that I considere youre beautee
And therwithal the unlikly elde of me,
I may nat, certes, though I sholde dye,
970 Forbere to been out of youre compaignye
For verray love; this is withouten doute.

Now kys me, wyf, and lat us rome aboute.'
   This fresshe May, whan she thise wordes herde,
Benyngnely to Januarie answerde,
975 But first and forward she bigan to wepe.
'I have,' quod she, 'a soule for to kepe
As wel as ye, and also myn honour,
And of my wyfhod thilke tendre flour,
Which that I have assured in youre hond,
980 Whan that the preest to yow my body bond;
Wherfore I wole answere in this manere,
By the leve of yow, my lord so deere:
I prey to God that nevere dawe the day
That I ne sterve, as foule as womman may,
985 If evere I do unto my kyn that shame,
Or elles I empeyre so my name,
That I be fals; and if I do that lak,
Do strepe me and put me in a sak,
And in the nexte ryver do me drenche.
990 I am a gentil womman and no wenche.
Why speke ye thus? But men been evere untrewe,
And wommen have repreve of yow ay newe.
Ye han noon oother contenance, I leeve,
But speke to us of untrust and repreeve.'
995   And with that word she saugh wher Damyan
Sat in the bussh, and coughen she bigan,
And with hir fynger signes made she
That Damyan sholde clymbe upon a tree
That charged was with fruyt, and up he wente.
1000 For verraily he knew al hire entente,
And every signe that she koude make,
Wel bet than Januarie, hir owene make,
For in a lettre she hadde toold hym al
Of this matere, how he werchen shal.
1005 And thus I lete hym sitte upon the pyrie,

And Januarie and May romynge myrie.
    Bright was the day, and blew the firmament;
Phebus hath of gold his stremes doun ysent
To gladen every flour with his warmnesse.
1010 He was that tyme in Geminis, as I gesse,
But litel fro his declynacion
Of Cancer, Jovis exaltacion.
And so bifel, that brighte morwe-tyde
That in that gardyn, in the ferther syde,
1015 Pluto, that is kyng of Fayerye,
And many a lady in his compaignye,
Folwynge his wyf, the queene Proserpyna,
Which that he ravysshed out of [Ethna]
Whil that she gadered floures in the mede –
1020 In Claudyan ye may the stories rede,
How in his grisely carte he hire fette –
This kyng of Fairye thanne adoun hym sette
Upon a bench of turves, fressh and grene,
And right anon thus seyde he to his queene:
1025 'My wyf,' quod he, 'ther may no wight seye nay;
Th'experience so preveth every day
The tresons whiche that wommen doon to man.
Ten hondred thousand [tales] tellen I kan
Notable of youre untrouthe and brotilnesse.
1030 O Salomon, wys, and richest of richesse,
Fulfild of sapience and of worldly glorie,
Ful worthy been thy wordes to memorie
To every wight that wit and reson kan.
Thus preiseth he yet the bountee of man:
1035 "Amonges a thousand men yet foond I oon,
But of wommen alle foond I noon."
    'Thus seith the kyng that knoweth youre
        wikkednesse.
And Jhesus, *filius Syrak*, as I gesse,

Ne speketh of yow but seelde reverence.
1040 A wylde fyr and corrupt pestilence
So falle upon youre bodyes yet to-nyght!
Ne se ye nat this honurable knyght,
By cause, allas, that he is blynd and old,
His owene man shal make hym cokewold.
1045 Lo, where he sit, the lechour, in the tree!
Now wol I graunten, of my magestee,
Unto this olde, blynde, worthy knyght
That he shal have ayen his eyen syght,
Whan that his wyf wold doon hym vileynye.
1050 Thanne shal he knowen al hire harlotrye,
Bothe in repreve of hire and othere mo.'
       'Ye shal?' quod Proserpyne, 'wol ye so?
Now by my moodres sires soule I swere
That I shal yeven hire suffisant answere,
1055 And alle wommen after, for hir sake,
That, though they be in any gilt ytake,
With face boold they shulle hemself excuse,
And bere hem doun that wolden hem accuse.
For lak of answere noon of hem shal dyen.
1060 Al hadde man seyn a thyng with bothe his yen,
Yit shul we wommen visage it hardily,
And wepe, and swere, and chyde subtilly,
So that ye men shul been as lewed as gees.
       'What rekketh me of youre auctoritees?
1065 I woot wel that this Jew, this Salomon,
Foond of us wommen fooles many oon.
But though that he ne foond no good womman,
Yet hath ther founde many another man
Wommen ful trewe, ful goode, and vertuous.
1070 Witnesse on hem that dwelle in Cristes hous;
With martirdom they preved hire constance.
The Romayn geestes eek make remembrance

Of many a verray, trewe wyf also.
But, sire, ne be nat wrooth, al be it so,
1075 Though that he seyde he foond no good womman,
I prey yow take the sentence of the man;
He mente thus, that in sovereyn bontee
Nis noon but God, but neither he ne she.
   'Ey! for verray God that nys but oon,
1080 What make ye so muche of Salomon?
What though he made a temple, Goddes hous?
What though he were riche and glorious?
So made he eek a temple of false goddis.
How myghte he do a thyng that moore forbode is?
1085 Pardee, as faire as ye his name emplastre,
He was a lecchour and an ydolastre,
And in his elde he verray God forsook;
And if God ne hadde, as seith the book,
Yspared him for his fadres sake, he sholde
1090 Have lost his regne rather than he wolde.
I sette right noght, of al the vileynye
That ye of wommen write, a boterflye!
I am a womman, nedes moot I speke,
Of elles swelle til myn herte breke.
1095 For sithen he seyde that we been jangleresses,
As evere hool I moote brouke my tresses,
I shal nat spare, for no curteisye,
To speke hym harm that wolde us vileynye.'
   'Dame,' quod this Pluto, 'be no lenger wrooth;
1100 I yeve it up! But sith I swoor myn ooth
That I wolde graunten hym his sighte ageyn,
My word shal stonde, I warne yow certeyn.
I am a kyng; it sit me noght to lye.'
   'And I,' quod she, 'a queene of Fayerye!
1105 Hir answere shal she have, I undertake.
Lat us namoore wordes heerof make;

For sothe, I wol no lenger yow contrarie.'
   Now lat us turne agayn to Januarie,
That in the gardyn with his faire May
1110 Syngeth ful murier than the papejay,
'Yow love I best, and shal, and oother noon.'
So longe aboute the aleyes is he goon,
Til he was come agaynes thilke pyrie
Where as this Damyan sitteth ful myrie
1115 An heigh among the fresshe leves grene.
   This fresshe May, that is so bright and sheene,
Gan for to syke, and seyde, 'Allas, my syde!
Now sire,' quod she, 'for aught that may bityde,
I moste han of the peres that I see,
1120 Or I moot dye, so soore longeth me
To eten of the smale peres grene.
Help, for hir love that is of hevene queene!
I telle yow wel, a womman in my plit
May han to fruyt so greet an appetit
1125 That she may dyen but she of it have.'
   'Allas,' quod he, 'that I ne had heer a knave
That koude clymbe! Allas, allas,' quod he,
'For I am blynd!' 'Ye, sire, no fors,' quod she;
'But wolde ye vouche sauf, for Goddes sake,
1130 The pyrie inwith youre armes for to take,
For wel I woot that ye mystruste me,
Thanne sholde I clymbe wel ynogh,' quod she,
'So I my foot myghte sette upon youre bak.'
   'Certes,' quod he, 'theron shal be no lak,
1135 Mighte I yow helpen with myn herte blood.'
He stoupeth doun, and on his bak she stood,
And caughte hire by a twiste, and up she gooth –
Ladyes, I prey yow that ye be nat wrooth;
I kan nat glose, I am a rude man –
1140 And sodeynly anon this Damyan

Gan pullen up the smok, and in he throng.
And whan that Pluto saugh this grete wrong,
To Januarie he gaf agayn his sighte,
And made hym se as wel as evere he myghte.
1145 And whan that he hadde caught his sighte agayn,
Ne was ther nevere man of thyng so fayn,
But on his wyf his thoght was everemo.
Up to the tree he caste his eyen two,
And saugh that Damyan his wyf had dressed
1150 In swich manere it may nat been expressed,
But if I wolde speke uncurteisly;
And up he yaf a roryng and a cry,
As dooth the mooder whan the child shal dye:
'Out! Help! Allas! Harrow!' he gan to crye,
1155 'O stronge lady stoore, what dostow?'
And she answerde, 'Sire, what eyleth yow?
Have pacience and resoun in youre mynde.
I have yow holpe on bothe youre eyen blynde.
Up peril of my soule, I shal nat lyen,
1160 As me was taught, to heele with youre eyen,
Was no thyng bet, to make yow to see,
Than strugle with a man upon a tree.
God woot, I dide it in ful good entente.'
'Strugle?' quod he, 'Ye, algate in it wente!
1165 God yeve yow bothe on shames deth to dyen!
He swyved thee; I saugh it with myne yen,
And elles be I hanged by the hals!'
'Thanne is,' quod she, 'my medicyne fals;
For certeinly, if that ye myghte se,
1170 Ye wolde nat seyn thise wordes unto me.
Ye han som glymsyng, and no parfit sighte.'
'I se,' quod he, 'as wel as evere I myghte,
Thonked be God! With bothe myne eyen two,
And by my trouthe, me thoughte he dide thee so.'

1175 'Ye maze, maze, goode sire,' quod she;
     'This thank have I for I have maad yow see.
     Allas,' quod she, 'that evere I was so kynde!'
        'Now, dame,' quod he, 'lat al passe out of mynde.
     Com doun, my lief, and if I have myssayd,
1180 God helpe me so, as I am yvele apayd.
     But, by my fader soule, I wende han seyn
     How that this Damyan hadde by thee leyn,
     And that thy smok hadde leyn upon his brest.'
        'Ye, sire,' quod she, 'ye may wene as yow lest.
1185 But, sire, a man that waketh out of his sleep,
     He may nat sodeynly wel taken keep
     Upon a thyng, ne seen it parfitly,
     Til that he be adawed verraily.
     Right so a man that longe hath blynd ybe,
1190 Ne may nat sodeynly so wel yse,
     First whan his sighte is newe come ageyn,
     As he that hath a day or two yseyn.
     Til that youre sighte ysatled be a while
     Ther may ful many a sighte yow bigile.
1195 Beth war, I prey yow, for by hevene kyng,
     Ful many a man weneth to seen a thyng,
     And it is al another than it semeth.
     He that mysconceyveth, he mysdemeth.'
     And with that word she leep doun fro the tree.
1200   This Januarie, who is glad but he?
     He kisseth hire and clippeth hire ful ofte,
     And on hire wombe he stroketh hire ful softe,
     And to his palays hoom he hath hire lad.
     Now, goode men, I pray yow to be glad.
1205 Thus endeth heere my tale of Januarie;
     God blesse us, and his mooder Seinte Marie!

Heere is ended the Marchantes Tale of Januarie.

Epilogue to the Merchant's Tale

'Ey! Goddes mercy!' seyde oure Hooste tho,
'Now swich a wyf I pray God kepe me fro!
Lo, whiche sleightes and subtilitees
1210 In wommen been! For ay as bisy as bees
Been they, us sely men for to deceyve,
And from the soothe evere wol they weyve;
By this Marchauntes tale it preveth weel.
But doutelees, as trewe as any steel
1215 I have a wyf, though that she povre be,
But of hir tonge, a labbyng shrewe is she,
And yet she hath an heep of vices mo;
Therof no fors! Lat alle swiche thynges go.
But wyte ye what? In conseil be it seyd,
1220 Me reweth soore I am unto hire teyd.
For and I sholde rekenen every vice
Which that she hath, ywis I were to nyce.
And cause why? It sholde reported be
And toold to hire of somme of this meynee –
1225 Of whom, it nedeth nat for to declare,
Syn wommen konnen outen swich chaffare;
And eek my wit suffiseth nat therto
To tellen al; wherfore my tale is do.'

Notes

The Merchant's portrait: General Prologue

The Merchant is described as well dressed and stylish, as befits his position as an apparently successful businessman. He talks knowledgeably about business, trade and currency exchange and, from his appearance, no one guesses he is in debt.

270 **forked berd**   This style of beard was very fashionable in the Middle Ages.

271 **mottelee**   cloth made up of various colours (again, very fashionable).

272 **Flaundryssh bever hat**   stylish hat originating from Flanders (in modern Belgium) made of beaver skin.

273 **clasped**   fastened.
     fetisly   elegantly.

274–5 He gave his opinions very solemnly, always relating to the increase of his profits.

276–7 He wanted the sea protected at all costs between Middelburgh (in Holland) and Orwell (on the English coast). This was a key trade route between Flanders and England, and important to the Merchant's business interests.

278 **sheeldes**   coins or units of monetary exchange.

279 **bisette**   employed, used.

280 No one knew that he was in debt.

281 **estatly**   dignified.
     governaunce   management.

282 **chevyssaunce**   financial arrangements.

284 **noot**   do not know. What do you think is the significance of this?

The Merchant's Prologue: Lines 1–32

The Merchant begins by echoing the words of the Clerk who had told the previous tale, which ended with the line:

And lat hym care, and wepe, and wrynge, and waille!

These seem fitting words to describe the Merchant's own experience of marriage. He tells the pilgrims that he knows all about the misery of marriage. He has only been married for two months but those two months have been far from happy; he tells his audience that his wife is the worst that there could be. He describes her as an ill-tempered, malicious and cruel woman. He is very clear that if he ever managed to escape the marriage he would never marry again. The Merchant experiences such pain even thinking about it that he will not go into further details but, at the Host's request, he agrees to tell a tale about marriage.

2 **on even and a-morwe**   night and day.
3 **other mo**   many more.
4 **trowe**   believe.
5 **woot**   know.
  fareth   goes.
7 Even if she was married to the devil.
8 **overmacche**   outdo.
9 **I yow reherce**   repeat to you.
10 **Hir hye malice**   her great spite.
   shrewe   bad-tempered woman.
   at al   in every way.
12 **Grisildis**   Griselda, the wife in *The Clerk's Tale* (noted for her great patience). See the illustration on page 93.
13 **passyng**   extreme.
14 **unbounden**   free (i.e. unmarried).
   also moot I thee   as I hope to prosper.
15 i.e. I would never marry again.
17 **Assaye whoso wole**   try it who will.

18 **Seint Thomas of Ynde**   Doubting Thomas, one of the disciples, who refused to believe in Jesus's resurrection until he had put his hands into the wounds Jesus had suffered at the crucifixion.

19–20 For most of us, I do not say for all, and God forbid that it be true.

21 **ywedded bee**   been married.

22 For no longer than two months, by God.

24–5 **ryve / Unto the herte**   tear apart his heart.

31–2 **but of myn... may namoore**   but of my own pain, because of my wounded heart I can say no more.

January and his desire to marry: Lines 33–54

The Merchant introduces the story of an elderly but wealthy knight from the city of Pavia in Lombardy. He has been single all his life but has now decided to marry. As a bachelor, he has always satisfied his sexual desires with women, but he now feels that he wants to experience the 'blissful life' that he believes exists between husband and wife.

33 **Whilom**   once.
   Lumbardye   Lombardy, a region in northern Italy.

35 **Pavye**   Pavia, in Italy.

36 And he had been single for 60 years.

37–8 And followed his sexual desire for women wherever his appetite led him.

39 **seculeer**   not in holy orders (and therefore not under a vow of chastity).

41 Either because of religious piety or old age.

42 **swich a greet corage**   such a great desire.

45 To see where he might be married (i.e. to find someone to marry).

47 **ones**   once.
   thilke   that same.

49–50 **that hooly boond... and womman bond**   Note the suggested link between the holy bond of matrimony and bondage. Note also the reference back to lines 14–15 in the Prologue, where the Merchant suggests marriage can ensnare a man.

51 No other life, he said, is worth a bean; i.e. marriage is the only worthwhile state.

52 **so esy and so clene**   so comfortable and morally pure.

53 **paradys**   Note the use of this word here, with its connotations of the Garden of Eden and the Fall. What does this suggest to you?

In praise of marriage: Lines 55–98

The Merchant interrupts his tale with a discussion about the positive aspects of married life. Whether these lines are meant to be taken as the thoughts of the Merchant or of January is unclear, and has given rise to some debate. The words are generally attributed to the Merchant but they do seem at odds with the views he gives in his Prologue on his own experience of marriage. It has been suggested that they are meant to be taken ironically.

He feels that it is a glorious thing to be married, especially if the man is older, as he will be more appreciative of the attentions of a loving, faithful wife. He rejects the ideas of scholars such as Theophrastus who, in his writings, warns against taking a wife at all as women can be motivated by greed and a desire to gain the possessions of their husband. Theophrastus feels wives do not really care about their husbands and are likely to be unfaithful. He claims that friends and servants are more reliable than wives.

55 **sooth**   true.

57 **hoor**   white-haired.

58 **fruyt of his tresor**   fruit of his treasure, i.e. something of great value to him.

59 **feir**   fair, beautiful.

60 **engendren hym an heir**   produce a son or heir.

61 **solas**   comfort.

63 **adversitee**   setback, problem.

64 **nys but childyssh vanytee**   is nothing but childish foolishness.

65 **it sit wel**　it is appropriate.

67–8 They build on unstable ground, and find instability when they believe it to be safe and solid.

69 **bryd**　bird.

70 Free and not in captivity.

71–2 Whereas a married man, in his position, lives a blissful and orderly life.

73 **yok**　yoke (harness used for horse and oxen). Marriage is likened to a yoke that binds people together, suggesting that they are unwilling partners and are put to labour and servitude.

74 **habounde**　abound (i.e. be plentiful).

75 **buxom**　obedient.

76 **eek**　also.

77 **syk and hool**　ill and well, i.e. in the words of the marriage ceremony 'in sickness and in health'.
make　partner.

78 She will stay with him through good and bad times.

79–80 She will not weary or tire of loving and serving him even if he is bedridden until he dies.

81 **clerkes**　scholars.

82 **Theofraste**　Theophrastus, an ancient Greek scholar who wrote *The Golden Book of Marriage*.
oon of tho　one of those.

83 What does it matter if Theophrastus wants to lie?

84 **for housbondrye**　for household economy.

85 To save money on household expenditure.

86 **dooth moore diligence**　works more diligently or conscientiously.

87 **Thy good to kepe**　to look after your possessions.

90 **verray freendes**　true friends.
knave　servant.

91–2 **she that waiteth ay / After thy good**　she that is always waiting to inherit your possessions.

93 **hoold**　keeping.

94 **Ful lightly maystow been**　very easily may you become.
cokewold　cuckold (i.e. a man whose wife is unfaithful to him).

95 **sentence**　opinion.

96 **corse**　curse.

97 But take no notice of such an empty idea.
98 **Deffie**   defy, i.e. ignore.

The benefits of having a wife: Lines 99–180

The Merchant continues to talk about the benefits of having a wife and the reasons why bachelorhood is an undesirable state. A wife is a blessing created by God and should be prized above all else. A wife is a man's companion and helper through good times and bad, and they are as one. He goes on to further extol the virtues of marriage and the bliss that exists between husband and wife, and tells his audience that a man should fall to his knees and give thanks to God for providing him with a wife, and pray also that she is with him to the very end of his life. He uses various authorities to support the view of marriage he has put forward. He cites the examples of figures from the Bible such as Jacob, Rebecca and Isaac, and the story of Judith. He also draws on the classical scholar, Cato, to further support his points.

99 **yifte**   gift.
     verraily   certainly.
100 **hardily**   assuredly.
101 **commune**   common land.
102 **moebles**   moveable possessions, personal property.
     yiftes of Fortune   i.e. dependent on chance or accident.
103 That pass like a shadow on a wall.
104 **drede nat**   do not fear.
105 A wife will last, and continue to live in your house.
106 **Wel lenger**   even longer.
     list   want.
107 **sacrement**   sacrament, i.e. important ritual in the Church.
108 **shent**   damned or ruined.
109 **desolat**   lonely.
110 **seculer estaat**   not in holy orders, i.e. not priests who would be expected to remain unmarried.
111 **I sey nat this for noght**   i.e. I mean this seriously.

112 **ywroght**   made.

118 **preve**   prove.

120 **terrestre**   earthly.
   disport   pleasure.

121–2 Note the qualities that Chaucer presents here – ones that May clearly lacks.

121 **buxom**   obedient, submissive.

123–4 One flesh they are and, I believe, one heart in happiness and sorrow. Note the echoes of biblical words on marriage.

125 **Seinte Marie**   Saint Mary (an exclamation).
   benedicite   bless us.

126–7 **How myghte... hath a wyf**   how can a man who has a wife have problems?

128 **bitwixe hem tweye**   between the two of them.

130 **povre**   poor.
   swynke   work.

131 **never a deel**   nothing at all.

132 **lust**   wants.
   hire liketh weel   she wants too.

133–4 Note the picture of complete obedience Chaucer creates here.

136 **murye**   merry.

138 **halt**   considers.

139–42 On his knees all his life should thank God for sending him a wife, or else pray to God to send him a wife to be with him until the end of his life.

143 **sikernesse**   security.

144 **gesse**   believe.

145 **werke after his wyves reed**   follows his wife's advice.

146 **beren up his heed**   hold his head up.

147–9 They are so faithful and wise, and if you too want to act wisely you will follow their advice.

150–53 The Book of Genesis relates that *Jacob*, on the advice of his mother Rebecca, used a goatskin to disguise himself as his elder brother Esau in order to trick his blind father into giving him his blessing.

151 **conseil**   counsel or advice.
   mooder   mother.

152 **Boond**   bound or tied.
   kydes skyn   skin of a young goat.

153 **fadres benyson** father's blessing.
   wan won.

154–6 According to the Book of *Judith*, the beautiful Hebrew widow seduced the invading general Holofernes (*Olofernus*), made him drunk, and then beheaded him. What do you make of the chosen examples of good women? See Interpretations pages 108–109.

156 **slow hym Olofernus** slew or killed Olofernus.

157 **Lo Abigayl… han be slayn** The first Book of Samuel relates how Abigail persuades King David to spare her husband *Nabal*, who has angered him.

159–62 **Ester also… enhaunced for to be** In the Old Testament, Esther pleaded with her husband, Ahasuerus, the Persian king, to promote her cousin Mordecai. See also 532–3.

161 **Mardochee** Mordecai.

162 **Of Assuere enhaunced** promoted by Ahasuerus.

163–4 There is nothing better, as Seneca says, than a humble wife. Seneca was a Roman philosopher and writer.

165 **Suffre** endure.
   Catoun Cato, a Roman statesman and writer.
   bit bade or instructed.

167 **obeye of curteisye** obey out of courtesy.

168 **kepere of thyn housbondrye** keeper or manager of your household.

169 **biwaille** bewail or lament.

170 **ther nys no wyf the hous to kepe** there is no wife to keep his house.

171 **if wisely thou wolt wirche** if you wish to act wisely.

174 **his flessh** According to Genesis, husband and wife become one flesh.

175 **fostreth** cares for or looks after.

176 **thee** thrive.

177 **what so men jape or pleye** whatever men say jokingly.

178 **holden the siker weye** keep to the safe path.

179 **knyt** united.
   bityde befall or happen to.

The Merchant returns to his story: Lines 181–256

The Merchant continues his story and explains how the knight, whose name is January, called his friends together to ask their advice about his plan to marry now that he is getting old. However, he tells them that he will not marry any woman over 20 years of age. Apart from being more desirable to him, he feels that young girls can be more easily controlled and moulded. He asks his friends to help prepare for his wedding as he intends to marry very soon. He will look for a suitable match himself, but also asks his friends to let him know if they see a likely candidate. To further support his desire to marry, he gives religious reasons such as having children and avoiding lechery.

182 **inwith his dayes olde**   in his old age.

183 **lusty**   happy, pleasant.

186 **th'effect of his entente**   what his intentions were.

187 **sad**   serious.

188 **hoor**   white-haired.

189 **on my pittes brynke**   on the edge of my grave (i.e. he is very old).

191 I have spent my life foolishly.

194 **anoon**   straightaway.

195 **mayde**   young woman, virgin.

196 **shapeth**   prepare.

197 **Al sodeynly**   immediately.

198 **wol fonde t'espien**   will try to find.

200 **forasmuche as**   insofar as.

201–2 He considers that his more powerful friends are in a better position to find a suitable woman for him to make an alliance with (marry).

203–4 But I warn you of one thing, my dear friends, there is no way I will have an old wife.

205 **passe**   be more than.

206 I prefer mature fish and young meat.

207 **pyk**   pike (large freshwater fish, often eaten in the Middle Ages).

pykerel   young pike.

208 **boef**   beef.

210 **bene-straw**   bean stalks.

forage   dried food for animals.

211 **eek thise olde wydwes**   also these old widows.

God it woot   God knows.

212–14 They are as crafty as Wade's boat, causing so much trouble wherever they please, so I would never have any rest with them. Wade is a figure from Anglo-Saxon legend, but the reference to his boat and its significance has now become obscure.

215 For many schools make subtle scholars. That is, women who have been married have learned cunning ways to handle husbands.

217 **a yong thyng may men gye**   a young woman can be more easily guided or controlled by a man.

218 **warm wex with handes plye**   mould warm wax in their hands.

219 **in a clause**   briefly.

220 **cause**   reason.

221 **were I hadde swich myschaunce**   if I was so unlucky.

223 **avoutrye**   adultery.

225 I could beget (conceive) no children with her**.**

226 I would rather be eaten by hounds.

227 **heritage**   property.

228 **straunge hand**   strangers' hands.

229 **I dote nat**   I am not in my dotage (senile).

232 **page**   page-boy, young servant.

234 **If he ne may nat**   if he is unable to.

235 **greet devocioun**   moral devotion.

236 **leveful procreacioun**   lawful procreation (having children within marriage).

237–8 **to th'onour... paramour or love**   Love-making is meant to produce children to honour God, not for sexual pleasure.

239 **leccherye eschue**   reject lechery.

240 And pay their debt when it is due. The matrimonial debt within the marriage contract involves the partners giving their bodies to each other.

241–3   Or each help the other when in trouble, like a sister and brother, and live a life of holy chastity.

245   **I dar make avaunt**   I dare boast.

246   **lymes**   limbs.
      stark and suffisaunt   strong and sufficient.

250   **blosmeth**   blossoms.
      er that fruyt ywoxen bee   before the fruit is grown.

253–4   My heart and all my limbs are as green as the laurel is seen throughout the year.

255   **syn**   since.
      myn entente   my intentions.

256   **assente**   agree (i.e. to help him).

January receives advice: Lines 257–364

Various friends advise January and give him their opinions, citing classical examples to support their points. An argument develops between Placebo (whose name means 'I will please'), who advises January to do what he thinks best, and Justinus ('the just person'), who is more critical of January's plan. Justinus warns January to be very cautious of who he shares his possessions and his life with, and cites the classical writer, Seneca, to support his views. January, though, dismisses the ideas of Seneca and the views of Justinus and declares that he will marry when and where he likes.

257   Different men told him different things.

258   **ensamples**   examples.

261   Arguments happen every day.

262   **disputisoun**   disagreement.

263–5   An argument began between two of his friends, one called Placebo and the other called Justinus (see headnote).

267   **Ful litel need hadde ye**   you had no need.

268   **Conseil to axe**   to ask advice.

269   **sapience**   wisdom.

271   To ignore the word of Solomon.

272   **everychon**   everyone.

273   **Wirk alle thyng by conseil**   do everything after taking advice.

274 **shaltow nat repente thee** you shall not be sorry.

279 **on me taak this motyf** take this advice from me.

280 **court-man** courtier.

282–3 I have held a high position with some very important lords.

284 Yet I never debated with them.

285 **contraried** contradicted.

286 **kan** knows.

287 **ferme and stable** i.e. true.

288 **semblable** similar.

289–92 Any counsellor who serves a high-ranking lord and yet presumes or thinks he is superior to him in knowledge is a fool.

293 **by my fay** by my faith.

295 **So heigh sentence** such good sense.

296–7 **I consente... opinioun** I agree and confirm everything you have said and the opinions you have given.

299 **Ne in Ytaille** nor in Italy.

300 Christ is very satisfied by this advice.

301 **an heigh corage** very brave.

302 **stapen is in age** is advanced in age.

303 **by my fader kyn** by my father's kin, or by my ancestors (an oath).

304 Your heart is happy.

305 **matiere** matter or business.

    leste choose or please.

310 Since you have spoken your mind, and listen to what I say.

312 Says that a man should listen carefully to advice.

313 **yeveth** gives.

    catel possessions, property (chattels).

314 **avyse me right wel** consider carefully.

317 **alwey** forever.

319 **avysement** careful consideration.

320 **enquere** investigate.

321 **dronkelewe** a heavy drinker, drunkard.

322 **shrewe** shrill and bad-tempered woman.

323 **chidestere** nagging, scolding woman.

    wastour extravagant spender (i.e. a waster of money).

324 **mannyssh wood** man-mad.

326 **trotteth hool in al** is perfect in every way (literally, 'trots soundly'). Note the horse image, suggesting that acquiring a good wife is like buying a horse.

330 More good qualities than bad vices.

331 **axeth leyser for t'enquere** requires leisure or time to consider.

333 **Ful pryvely** privately.

334 Let him who wishes praise married life (i.e. no matter who praises married life).

336 **observances** duties.
of alle blisses bare lacking in all happiness.

338 **route** crowd.

339 **stedefast** faithful.

340 **mekeste** meekest.

341 I know best where my shoe pinches.

342 You may, as far as I'm concerned, please yourself what you do.

343 **Avyseth yow** think carefully.

347 **route** company.

348 **Is bisy ynough** has enough to do.

349 **To han his wyf allone** to keep his wife to himself.

352 **many an observaunce** much attention.

353 **yvele apayd** dissatisfied or displeased.

355 I don't give a straw for your Seneca or for your proverbs.

356–7 **I counte nat... scole-termes** your scholarly references are not worth a basket of herbs.

358 **assenteden** agreed.

361 **letteth matrimoigne** hinders marriage.
sickerly certainly.

January chooses his wife: Lines 365–476

January has many fantasies about a prospective bride, and considers many possible options. Eventually he decides on his bride-to-be and informs his friends of his decision; he does not want to hear any arguments against it. He has chosen a beautiful young woman from the town, although she is from a family of low social status. He has one worry, though, which he tells his friends about: he has heard that no one can live in bliss in both this world and in heaven. He is worried that if he has a blissful marriage he will lose the chance of attaining a blessed state in heaven later.

Justinus dismisses this as nonsense, and jokingly comments that God could perform a miracle to make marriage a kind of purgatory if this were the case. More seriously, he warns January that it is best to live a life of moderation and avoid sin, drawing his comments to a close by reminding him that the Wife of Bath has already given them a clear picture of what marriage is really like in her view.

365–7 Every day, January's thoughts were filled with fantasies and wild imaginings about his marriage.

368–9 Many shapely figures and beautiful faces came into his thoughts each night.

370–73 **As whoso... By his mirour** As if someone took a mirror, polished bright, placed it in the common marketplace and watched the many figures that pass by.

374 **Gan** did.
inwith in.
devyse think about.

376 He did not know which one to choose.

378 **stant** stood.

379 **sadnesse** seriousness and steadfastness.
benyngnytee graciousness.

380 Among the people she had the best reputation.

382 **bitwixe ernest and game** part in earnest and part in fun.

383 **apoynted** decided.

385 And chose her on his own authority.

386 **alday** always.

387 When he was in bed (literally, when he was brought or taken to bed).

388 **purtreyed** imagined.

390 Her slim waist, her long slender arms.

391 **governaunce** behaviour, demeanour.
gentillesse noble character.

392 **berynge** bearing.
sadnesse serious manner.

393 **on hire was condescended** had decided on her.

394 He felt his choice could not be bettered.

396 He thought everyone else's views were so bad.

397–8 **repplye / Agayn**   criticize.

399 **instaunce**   request.

402 **abregge hir labour**   shorten their work.

403–4 There was no need for them to search any further; he had made his choice and he would stick to it.

406 **alderfirst... boone**   first of all he asked them all a favour.

410 **verray ground**   true foundation.

413 Even though she was of low rank.

414 **Suffiseth hym**   it was sufficient for him.

416 To lead a life of ease and holiness.

417 **han hire al**   possess her completely.

418 That no person would part him from his joy.

419–20 And asked them to help him in his need and ensure that he did not fail to be successful.

424 **reherce**   speak about.

425 **ful yoore ago**   a long time ago.

426 No man may have two kinds of perfect bliss.

428 **kepe hym fro the synnes sevene**   keep himself clear of the seven sins. In the Middle Ages, the Seven Deadly Sins were often depicted as a tree, with the branches symbolizing the various sins (see 429).

430 **parfit felicitee**   perfect happiness.

431 **ese and lust**   pleasure and delight.

434 **delicat**   delightful, pleasing.

436–40 Here, the Merchant says he is worried that in order to get into heaven he should suffer and pay penance in life. He wonders how he can live in such pleasure and hope to attain heaven and eternal life after he dies.

442 **Assoilleth**   solve, answer.

443 **folye**   foolishness.

444 Answered straight away in mockery.

445 **abregge**   shorten.

446 **auctoritee**   authority (i.e. writer supported by classical scholars).

449 **wirche**   work.

450 **er ye have... chirche**   before you receive the last rites from the Church (i.e. before you die).

453 **elles**   otherwise.
      sente   should send.

455 **Wel ofte**   much more often.
456 **reed I kan**   advice I know.
457 **Dispeire yow noght**   do not despair.
458 **Paraunter**   perhaps.
    purgatorie   purgatory.
459 **meene**   instrument, means.
461 **arwe**   arrow.
463–5 There is not so much happiness in marriage, nor ever shall be, that it will prevent you from receiving salvation.
466–7 Provided that you use moderation in enjoying the pleasure of your wife.
470 **my wit is thynne**   my knowledge is limited.
471 **Beth nat agast herof**   don't worry about it.
472 But let's wade out of this matter (i.e. let's leave the subject).
473–5 The Wife of Bath, if you have understood her, has described marriage very well and briefly.

January is married: Lines 477–529

January's friends accept his decision and, as January is intent on marrying quickly, help to make arrangements for the wedding and the drawing up of the wedding contract. January's marriage takes place and is followed by a very grand and elaborate wedding feast, with music accompanying every course.

477 **Justyn**   i.e. Justinus.
478 Took their leave of January and each other.
480 They carefully and wisely made an agreement.
481 **which that Mayus highte**   who was called May.
482 As quickly as she possibly could.
484 **trowe**   believe.
485 **scrit and bond**   document and pledge.
486 **feffed in his lond**   endowed with his land.
487 Or have you listen to a description of her rich garments.
490 **hooly sacrement**   holy sacrament (of marriage).
491 **stole**   long, narrow piece of decorated cloth a priest wears around his neck.

492 And bade her to be like Sarah and Rebecca (wives in the Bible noted for their wisdom and faithfulness).

494 **orisons**   prayers.

495 **croucheth hem**   blessed them with the sign of the cross.

496 And made all secure in holiness (i.e. they were securely bound together through religious ceremonies).

499 **deys**   dais, raised platform where the top table is placed.

500 **paleys**   palace.

501 **instrumentz**   musical instruments.
    vitaille   food.

502 The most dainty in the whole of Italy.

504 **Orpheus**   In mythology, *Orpheus* – the son of Apollo – was a legendary harp-player.
    of Thebes Amphioun   Amphion, king of Thebes (another legendary harp-player).

505 Never made such a melody.

506 **cours**   course (of the banquet).
    mynstralcye   music and singing.

507–9 Joab's trumpets did not sound more clearly, nor were those of Theodamus half so clear when the city of Thebes was in danger of falling.

510 **Bacus**   Bacchus, the Greek god of wine.
    shynketh   pours out.

511 **Venus**   the goddess of love.

513 **assayen his corage**   test his courage.

514 As a bachelor and also in marriage.

515 **fyrbrond**   fire-brand. Venus is pictured as leading the dance, holding a flaming torch.

516 **al the route**   all the company.

518 **Ymeneus**   Hymen, the god of marriage.

520 **Marcian**   Marcianus Capella, a Roman poet who wrote on marriage.

521–3 Who wrote about the merry wedding of Philology and Mercury, and of the songs the Muses sang.

524–5 Your pen and your tongue are too small to depict this marriage.

526 **stoupyng**   stooping, bent.

528 **Assayeth it**   try it.
    witen   find out.

May gains an admirer: Lines 530–582

January's new bride, May, is young and beautiful and he is entranced every time he looks at her face. He begins to fantasize about what will happen that night and he becomes eager for his guests to leave, so he tactfully tries to hurry them along. Eventually, everyone begins to depart, happy for January and May, all except for one young man, a squire named Damyan who has fallen in love with May. He is so love-struck that he is suffering greatly, and he retires to bed to consider what he can do about his situation. The Merchant here gives his audience an indication that this young squire will present a threat to January's happiness.

530 **so benyngne a chiere**   so benign a facial expression.

531 To see her seemed like something out of a fairy tale.

532–3 Even Queen Esther did not have such a meek look in her eye when she captivated King Ahasuerus with her beauty. (The Old Testament's Book of Esther tells how her beauty and her apparent meekness captivated her husband, King Ahasuerus.)

534 **devyse**   describe.

536 **morwe**   morning.

538 **ravysshed in a traunce**   sent into a trance (captivated by her beauty).

540 In his heart he began to menace her. See Interpretations pages 98–99 for a discussion of these lines.

541 **in armes wolde hire streyne**   in his arms he would hold (or constrain) her.

542 **Parys dide Eleyne**   In Greek mythology, Paris abducted Helen of Troy, an act that resulted in the Trojan War.

544 That he must offend her that night.

546–7 God grant that you may endure my sharp and hot sexual desires.

548 **agast**   afraid.

549 God forbid that I should use all my strength and desire.

550 **woxen**   become.

552 **ago**   gone.

555 **mete**   food.
     in subtil wyse   discreetly.

556 **resoun was to ryse**   it was reasonable to leave the table.

558 And they went round the house scattering spices in every room.
560 **Al but** except for.
   squyer squire, young man training to be a knight.
   highte Damyan called Damyan.
561 **carf biforn** carved before (carved the meat for his master and served him).
563 **verray peyne** great pain (of love).
   ny wood nearly mad.
564 He almost perished and fainted where he stood.
565 So sorely had Venus hurt him with her brand.
566 **bar it** bore it, carried it.
570 **rewen on** take pity on.
571 **bedstraw** straw used to stuff a mattress.
   bredeth breeds (i.e. spreads or starts).
572 **famulier foo** familiar foe (i.e. a false friend).
   bedeth waits.
573 **false hoomly hewe** false household servant.
574 **naddre** adder (poisonous snake).
576 **dronken in plesaunce** drunk with pleasure.
578 **thy borne man** a man born to serve you.
581 **pestilence** plague.
582 **hoomly foo** familiar foe (i.e. within the household).

January takes May to bed: Lines 583–653

Finally January's long-awaited moment arrives and, after toasts have been drunk, his friends bring May to his bed. Now alone, January embraces May, apologizing for any roughness in his lovemaking but assuring her that, now they are married, nothing they do will be sinful as she is his wife. He also apologizes if his lovemaking seems slow, but they have all the time they want and a workman does a job better if it is done slowly.

The Merchant's description of January here is not at all flattering, and he conjectures what May must have thought of him. January's lovemaking continues through the night and at dawn he breaks into discordant song. January then goes to sleep, but May stays alone in her room, as is customary for a bride, for the next four days.

583 The sun had completed its daily arc (i.e. it was sunset).

584–5 No longer could his (the sun's) body linger on the horizon in that latitude.

586 **mantel** cloak.

  rude rough.

588 **lusty route** merry crowd.

591 Where they do as they please.

593 **hastif** hasty.

595 **ypocras, clarree, and vernage** Hippocras is a spiced cordial drink; *clarree* is wine with honey and spices, and *vernage* is a strong sweet wine.

596 **t'encreessen his corage** to increase his desire.

597 **letuarie** drug, medicine.

598 **the cursed monk, daun Constantyn** Constantinus was an eleventh-century monk and doctor from Carthage. *Daun* is an academic title.

599 *De Coitu* literally 'On Sex'.

600 He was not averse to swallowing all of them.

601 **privee** close.

603 **Lat voyden** empty.

  in curteys wyse as courteously as possible.

605 Men drank a toast and the curtains were drawn.

608 Everybody left the room.

610 **make** mate.

611 **lulleth** soothed, caressed.

613 **houndfyssh** dogfish.

  brere briar. What is the effect of these terms?

616 **moot trespace** must offend or do wrong.

618 Before I go to sleep.

622 **at leyser parfitly** in a leisurely way, perfectly.

623 **It is no fors** it doesn't matter.

624 In true wedlock we two are joined.

625 **yok that we been inne** yoke that we are in. Note how the image of them being harnessed together is created here.

626 **mowe** may.

629 **leve** leave, permission.

630 **day gan dawe** day began to dawn.

631 **a sop in fyn clarree** bread dipped in a fine wine.

634 **made wantown cheere** behaved in a wanton mood.

635 **coltissh**   frisky (like a colt).
   ragerye   passion.
636 **jargon**   chatter.
   flekked pye   magpie.
637 **slakke**   slack or loose.
638 **chaunteth**   sings.
   craketh   croaks.
641 **nekke lene**   lean neck.
642 She did not praise his playing and did not think it worth a bean.
645 **pryme**   first part of the day (i.e. from about 6 to 9 am).
648 Stayed in her room until the fourth day.
649 **As usage is of wyves**   as is customary for wives.

January sends May to Damyan: Lines 654–742

The Merchant's narrative now switches to Damyan, who we last saw retiring to his room sick for love of May. He is so consumed by passion for her that he must find a way of letting her know how he feels. To this end he writes a letter, which he keeps in a silk purse hanging under his shirt next to his heart. Meanwhile, on the fourth day May leaves her room and joins January.

January has noticed the absence of his squire and asks the other squires where he is; they tell him that Damyan is ill. January is sorry to hear that and decides to visit him after he has eaten, intending to take May with him. However, January changes his mind and tells May to go and visit Damyan with some of her women first, and he will visit later after he has had a rest. During May's visit, Damyan secretly gives her the purse containing his letter and whispers to her not to reveal it to anyone. May returns to January who is still in bed. She makes the excuse of wanting to go to the toilet, where she reads Damyan's letter before tearing it up and throwing it into the lavatory.

655 **langwissheth**   languishes.
657 **sely**   foolish.
658 **Andswere to my demaunde**   answer my question, tell me this.

659 **shaltow**   shall you.

661 **she wol thy wo biwreye**   she will betray your sorrow.

663 **sike**   sick.

664 **brenneth**   burns.

665 **in aventure**   at risk.

667 **penner**   writing case.

669 **a compleynt or a lay**   a poetic lament (usually on the subject of unrequited love) or a song.

671 **purs**   purse.

673–5 The moon, which had been in the second house of Taurus at noon on the day when January married May, had now glided into Cancer. (See the illustration of zodiac signs on page 121.)

682 **heighe masse**   high mass (main religious service of the day).

684 Note the sense of brightness and steadfastness usually associated with May.

688 **entendeth nat to me**   does not attend on me.

689 **how may this bityde**   how has this come about.

690–91 The other squires who waited on January told him that Damyan was ill.

692 **letted hym to doon his bisynesse**   prevented him from doing his job.

693 **tarye**   delay.

694 **forthynketh**   causes regret.

696 **deyde**   died.

697 **secree**   secret.

699 **servysable**   capable.

700 **thrifty**   useful.

701 **after mete**   after dinner.

704–7 And for these words every man blessed him for his goodness and nobility in comforting his sick squire, because it was a kind deed.

712 **Dooth hym disport**   entertain him.

714 After I have had a little rest.

715–16 And hurry back, because I will wait until you come back and sleep by my side.

718 **marchal of his halle**   master of ceremonies.

720 **hath streight hir wey yholde**   went straight away.

724 **whan that his tyme he say**   when he saw the right moment.

725 Secretly his purse and also his letter.

726 **wille**   wishes, desires.

727 **withouten moore** with nothing more (i.e. without explanation).

728 **siketh wonder depe and soore** sighed very deeply and sorrowfully.

730 **discovere me** give me away.

731 **kyd** made known.

733 **ye gete namoore of me** you will get no more from me. The Merchant chooses not to comment on Damyan's action or May's response. Why, do you think?

735 **ful softe** very quietly.

738–9 **She feyned… moot neede** she pretended that she must go where, as you know, everyone must go (i.e. she pretended that she wanted to go to the toilet).

741 **rente it al to cloutes** tore it into pieces.

742 And quietly threw it into the latrine.

May is in love with Damyan: Lines 743–808

May goes back to bed, where January is still asleep, but her mind keeps going over Damyan's letter. When January wakes he begs May to take all her clothes off, but the Merchant will not describe more of this moment for fear of offending the more sensitive members of his audience. May, however, cannot get Damyan out of her mind and takes pity on him, promising herself that she will love him more than anyone even though he is poor. To set things in motion, May writes a letter to Damyan, promising that she will be his if they can only arrange a suitable time and place where they can be alone together. May takes her letter to Damyan the next time she visits him and secretly leaves it under his pillow. She squeezes his hand, wishes him well and returns to January, who has called for her. The next morning, Damyan gets up, his sickness and sorrow completely gone, and goes to see January confident that he is in May's favour.

743 **studieth** pondered, thought carefully.

747 He wanted, he said, to have some pleasure with her.

749 **be hire lief or looth**   whether she liked it or not.

750 **precious**   fastidious or prudish.

751 **How that he wroghte**   what he did.

753–4 But here I leave them working as they wished until evensong rang and they must arise.

755–8 Whether it was by fate or chance or nature, or some influence of the stars, that the heavens were at that time in a fortunate aspect.

759 **a bille of Venus werkes**   a document of Venus's works. That is, it was a good time to begin a love affair.

760 **alle thyng hath tyme**   there is a time for everything.

764 **deme**   judge.
   holde my pees   hold my peace (i.e. keep quiet).

765 **sooth**   truth.

766–7 Had received such an impression that day which made her pity this love-sick Damyan.

768 **she ne dryve kan**   she cannot drive.

771 **rekke noght**   do not care.
   I hym assure   I promise him.

774 **pitee renneth soone in gentil herte**   pity flows swiftly in a kind heart.

775–6 Here you may see how excellent the generosity is in women who think carefully about things.

777 There may be such a tyrant.

779 **sterven**   die (i.e. of unrequited love).

782 And not care about being a murderer.

785 **verray grace**   true favour (i.e. she agreed to love him).

786 **Ther lakketh noght**   nothing was lacking.

787 **unto his lust suffise**   satisfy his desires.

791 **sotilly**   craftily, stealthily.

793 She took his hand and squeezed it hard.

795 **bad hym been al hool**   bade him get better.

799 He combed his hair, preened and groomed himself.

802 **bowe**   bone.

804 For cunning is everything, for those who can use it.

805 **speke hym good**   speak well of him.

January is struck by blindness: Lines 809–919

The Merchant now describes the luxury of January's life, living as if he were a king. One of the things he possesses is a beautiful walled garden, finer than any other. He wants to keep this garden for the exclusive use of himself and May, and only he holds a key for its small gate. In the summer he likes to make love to May in the garden. However, the Merchant points out that worldly joy does not last and, inexplicably, January is suddenly struck blind. Understandably he is grief stricken, but his torment is made worse because of his jealousy that May might be tempted by another man. Eventually, after a month or two, his sorrow begins to lessen when he comes to terms with the fact that nothing can be done about the loss of his sight.

His feelings of jealousy about May do not diminish, though, and he will not allow his wife to go anywhere without him, day or night. Both May and Damyan are upset by this as they cannot speak to each other without January hearing. However, they do find a way to communicate through letters and signs, and May manages to make a wax impression of the key to the garden gate. Knowing what she has in mind, Damyan has a copy of the key made. The Merchant indicates that the audience will hear more about this key, and he reminds them how love will always find a way.

810 **Stant in delit**   lies in sensual pleasure.
812 **as longeth to**   as is expected for.
813 Planned to live in pleasure.
815 According to his social rank as a king's are.
818 I know of no other garden so beautiful.
820 **Romance of the Rose**   French allegorical romance which
     Chaucer had helped to translate into English. The poem is set in
     a Garden of Love.
821 Could not have imagined its beauty.
822 **Priapus**   god of fertility. Note the association between the
     natural growth in the garden and the idea of sexual love.

825 **under a laurer alwey grene**   under an evergreen laurel. Note the repetition of the laurel image, used by January to describe himself in line 254.

826 **Pluto**   classical god of the Underworld. He abducted *Proserpina* and took her to Hades where she lived as his queen, becoming the goddess of spring and fertility. (Note the suggested parallel between January and May.)

827 **al hire fayerye**   all her fairies.

828 **Disporten**   played.

831 **deyntee**   delight.

832 That he would not allow anyone to have a key.

833 **smale wyket**   narrow gate.

834 **clyket**   key.

835 **he it unshette**   he unlocked it.

836 **dette**   (marital) debt.

839 And anything they had not done in bed.

840 **spedde**   succeeded.

843 **dure**   last, endure.

845 **sodeyn hap**   sudden chance happening.

846 **scorpion**   The *scorpion* was a symbol of treachery.
   deceyvable   deceitful.

848 **envenymynge**   poisoning.

849 O brittle joy! O venom sweet and strange!

850 **peynte**   paint, i.e. disguise.

851 **hewe**   colour (i.e. disguise).
   stidefastnesse   steadfastness, constancy.

855 **biraft hym bothe his yen**   deprived him of both his eyes.

856 For the grief of which he wished to die.

858 **lust**   pleasure.

859 **woxen**   become.

862 In case his wife should do something foolish.

863 **brente**   burnt.

865–8 For neither after his death nor during his lifetime did he want her to be the lover or wife of anyone else, but to forever live in the black clothes of the widow, alone, like the turtle dove that has lost her mate.

870 **gan aswage**   began to lessen.

871 For when he saw that things could not be any other way.

873–4 Save that, without a doubt, he could not stop his constant jealousy.

875 **outrageous** excessive.

876–7 **That neither... oother place** that neither at home, nor in any other house, nor in any other place.

878 **suffre hire** allow her.

879 Unless his hand was always on her.

881 **benyngnely** graciously.

882–3 That she must either die immediately or else have him as she desired.

884 She expected her heart would burst.

889 **purpos** intentions.

of no swich mateere there was no chance.

893 **privee signes** private signals.

wiste he what she mente he knew what she meant.

894 **fyn** end, outcome.

897–8 For the blind can be deceived just the same as those who can see.

899 **Argus** a hundred-eyed giant killed by Hermes in Greek mythology.

900 **poure or pryen** peer or gaze.

901 **blent** blind (i.e. deceived).

902 **wenen wisly that it be nat so** confidently suppose that it is not so (i.e. that they are not deceived).

903 **Passe over is an ese** to overlook or ignore something is the easy way.

904 **so yoore** before.

909 **countrefeted pryvely** secretly copied.

911 Some wondrous event, involving this key, will happen.

913 **Ovyde** Roman poet who wrote the love story of Pyramus and Thisbe.

ful sooth seystou what you say is very true.

914–15 There is no cunning trick, no matter how longstanding or intense, that love will not find a way to overcome.

916 **Piramus and Tesbee** Pyramus and Thisbe. In Ovid's story Pyramus and Thisbe are lovers who are kept strictly apart but manage to communicate with each other by whispering through a crack in a wall, and make plans to elope. The story, however, does not end happily.

79

917 **kept ful longe streite overal**   kept strictly constrained for a
   long time (i.e. they were kept apart and strictly watched).
918 **rownynge**   whispering.
919 No one would have thought of that trick.

May promises to be true, and Damyan hides in the tree: Lines 920–1006

As June begins, May encourages January to visit the garden and
he eagerly takes up her suggestion. May gives Damyan a look that
signals to him she wants him to go and hide himself in the garden.
January takes May to the garden, tells her how much he loves her
and that he will give her all he has. May, in return, promises that she
will always be faithful to him. She asks him why he should doubt her
when it is men who are the unfaithful ones. As she is speaking, she
sees Damyan close by and signals to him that he should climb a tree
while January and May walk in the garden.

923 **Thurgh eggying of his wyf**   through the encouragement of his
   wife.
924 **no wight but they tweye**   just the two of them.
927 **The turtles voys**   the voice of the turtle dove.
928 **reynes weete**   wet rains.
929 **eyen columbyn**   eyes like a dove.
934 **spot**   stain or blemish (in a moral sense).
935 **disport**   pleasure.
937 **lewed**   ignorant, stupid.
941 **stirte**   rushed, went quickly.
942 **no wight myghte it se neither yheere**   no one might see or
   hear.
947 **clapte to**   shut, closed.
951 I would rather die on a knife.
953 **chees**   chose.
954 **coveitise**   covetousness, greed.
957 **Beth to me trewe**   be true to me.
960 **al myn heritage**   all my inheritance.

      toun and tour   town and tower.
961 **chartres**   contracts, legally binding documents.
962 **er sonne reste**   before sunset.
963 **wisly**   truly.
965 **wyte me noght**   do not blame me.
968 **unlikly**   unsuitable.
      elde   old age.
970 **Forbere**   endure.
972 **rome aboute**   roam or wander about.
975 **first and forward**   first of all.
978–80 And my wifehood is like a tender flower which I entrusted to
      your hands when the priest bound my body to you. (May is
      reminding January of the wedding vows that she made to him.)
984 Or let me die as foully as a woman can.
986 **empeyre**   impair or harm.
988 **strepe**   strip.
989 **drenche**   drown.
992 And women are always blamed by men.
993–4 You have no way of behaving other than speaking of mistrust
      and blame.
1002 **make**   mate.
1004 **how he werchen shal**   how he should act.
1005 **pyrie**   pear tree.

Pluto and Proserpina intervene: Lines 1007–1107

The Merchant digresses from his tale as he imagines Pluto, the King of Fairyland, and his queen Proserpina, who are also present in the garden, discussing the infidelity of women. Pluto says that their infidelities are recorded in thousands of tales, and he cites evidence from the Bible to support his arguments. His attention then switches to Damyan, *the lechour*, sitting in the tree, waiting for May, who is intent on deceiving her husband. Pluto says he will restore the old knight's sight the instant that May starts her infidelity with Damyan. Proserpina replies that she will inspire May with an excuse that will explain to January what is happening, and will disguise her guilt. She takes May's side, and the side of womankind in general, and rejects Pluto's view, citing her own evidence of the faithfulness of women. Pluto and Proserpina make peace with each other, with Pluto intent on restoring January's sight and Proserpina determined to ensure May can devise an explanation for her behaviour.

1007 **blew the firmament**   the sky was blue.

1008 **Phebus**   Phoebus, the sun.

1010 **in Geminis**   in the sign of Gemini.

1111–12 **declynacion / Of Cancer**   declining into the sign of Cancer.

1112 **Jovis exaltacion**   with Jupiter in its strongest influence.

1013 **bifel**   occurred, happened.

1014 **in the ferther syde**   at the far side.

1018–19 In Greek mythology Pluto, the ruler of the Underworld, had abducted Proserpina and carried her away while she was picking flowers on the slopes of Mount Etna.

1020 **Claudyan**   Claudius Claudianus, a fourth-century writer who wrote *De Raptu Proserpinae* (*The Rape of Proserpina*).

1021 **grisely**   frightening, grim.

1023 **turves**   turfs.

1025 **no wight seye nay**   no one deny it.

1026 **preveth**   proves.

1027 **tresons**   betrayals.

1029 **brotilnesse**   fickleness.

1030 **Salomon**   Solomon, an Old Testament king who had many wives and was noted for his wisdom.

1031 **Fulfild of sapience**   endowed with much wisdom.

1032–3 Your words are very memorable to every person capable of reason.

1034 **bountee**   goodness, virtue.

1035–6 Among a thousand men I found one, but not one in all women.

1038 **Jhesus, *filius Syrak***   Jesus, son of Syrak (not Jesus Christ, but the supposed author of the Book of Ecclesiasticus).

1039 Rarely speaks of you with respect.

1040 **corrupt pestilence**   foul infectious disease, plague.

1042 **Ne se ye nat**   do you not see.

1044 His own servant will make him a cuckold.

1045 The Merchant here reminds his audience of Damyan (*the lechour*) still sitting in the pear tree.

1048 **have ayen his eyen syght** once more have his sight.

1049 **wold doon hym vileynye** wants to do him harm (i.e. betray him).

1050 **harlotrye** wickedness, looseness.

1051 Both to reprove her and others as well.

1052 **wol ye so** is that what you want.

1054 **suffisant** adequate, suitable.

1056 **in any gilt ytake** caught in any guilty situation.

1057 They will excuse themselves with a bold-faced explanation.

1058 **bere hem doun** overcome those.

1060–61 Even if a man has seen something with his own eyes, we women shall give a bold explanation to excuse ourselves.

1063 **lewed as gees** gullible as geese.

1064 What do I care about your authorities?

1066 Found many fools among us women.

1067–9 But if he never found a woman who was true there are many men who have found them faithful, good and virtuous.

1070 **Cristes hous** i.e. heaven.

1072 **Romayn geestes** Roman stories.

1074 **ne be nat wrooth, al be it so** do not be angry, even if it is so.

1076 **sentence** opinion, meaning.

1077 **sovereyn bontee** supreme goodness.

1079–80 God knows that Solomon is only one, so why do you make so much of Solomon?

1084 **that moore forbode is** that is more forbidden.

1085–6 Truly, as much as you gloss over his reputation, he was a lecher and idolater.

1087 **elde** old age.
forsook abandoned.

1088 **ne hadde** had not.

1089 **Yspared** spared.

1090 Have lost his kingdom sooner than he wanted.

1091–2 I set at nothing, less than a butterfly, all the wicked things you write about women.

1095 **jangleresses** chatterers, gossips.

1096–8   As long as I keep my hair (i.e. live) I will not refrain out of
          politeness from speaking ill against he who says wicked things
          about us.
1099   **wrooth**   angry.
1103   **it sit me noght to lye**   it is not fitting for me to lie.
1107   **I wol no lenger yow contrarie**   I will no longer contradict you.

May and Damyan make love: Lines 1108–1141

The Merchant returns his attention to May and Damyan, as May begins to put her plan into operation. She tells January that she is in pain and that she must eat one of the pears that she can see in the tree to satisfy her craving. She hints that this sudden craving is linked to pregnancy. January is eager to satisfy her desire for a pear, but there is no one else around to climb the tree to pick one for her, so she asks January to put his arms around the tree trunk so she can climb on his back and go into the tree herself. Once she is up in the tree, Damyan hastily pulls up her smock and begins to make love to her.

1110   **papejay**   parrot.
1112   **aleyes**   garden paths.
1113   **come agaynes thilke pyrie**   came near this pear tree.
1116   **sheene**   shining, radiant.
1117   **syke**   sigh.
         Allas, my syde   i.e. she has a pain in her side.
1118   **for aught that may bityde**   whatever happens.
1119   **han of the peres**   have one of the pears.
1123   **a womman in my plit**   a woman in my condition. May is
         implying that she is pregnant.
1126–7   **that I ne... koude clymbe**   that I don't have a servant here who
         could climb the tree.
1128   **no fors**   it doesn't matter.
1130   To put your arms around the trunk of the pear tree.
1137   **twiste**   branch.

1138 **wrooth** angry.
1139 **glose** gloss over, cover up.
     rude plain.
1141 Pulled up her smock and thrust in.

January's sight is restored: Lines 1142–1206

Pluto immediately gives January back his sight, and January sees what Damyan is up to with his wife. January gives a loud cry and begins to shout to them, asking them what they are doing. May tells him that she has helped to get his sight back as she had been told that there was no better cure for his blindness than for her to struggle with a man in a tree. January is not entirely convinced, but she tells him that when someone has their sight restored, at first the vision is imperfect, and it will take a while for him to see things clearly. She comes down from the tree and January kisses her and takes her back to his palace.

1143 **gaf** gave.
1146 Never was a man so pleased about anything.
1149 **dressed** treated.
1151 **uncurteisly** crudely.
1152–3 He gave out a roaring and crying like a mother when her child dies.
1154 **Harrow** help.
1155 O bold, brazen lady, what are you doing?
1156 **what eyleth yow** what's wrong with you.
1158 I have helped you regain your sight.
1160–62 I was told that to heal your eyes there was nothing better than to struggle with a man in a tree.
1163 **in ful good entente** with the best of intentions.
1164 **algate in it wente** it went in completely.
1166 **He swyved thee** he had sex with you.
1167 **hals** neck.
1169 **if that ye myghte se** if you could truly see.

1171 **glymsyng**   impaired vision.
1175 **maze**   are confused, bewildered.
1176 This is all the thanks I get for helping you to see again.
1178 **lat al passe out of mynde**   let's forget about it all.
1179 **my lief**   my dear.
1180 **I am yvele apayd**   I've paid the price, been punished for it.
1181 **I wende han seyn**   I thought I saw.
1182 **by thee leyn**   lain by you.
1183 **thy smok hadde leyn upon his brest**   your smock had lain on his chest.
1184 **ye may wene as yow lest**   you must think what you like.
1186 **wel taken keep**   fully understand, grasp.
1188 **adawed verraily**   fully awake.
1190 **yse**   see.
1193 **ysatled**   settled down.
1194 There may be many sights that deceive you.
1195 **Beth war**   beware, be careful.
1196 **weneth**   believes.
1198 He that misunderstands, misjudges.
1201 **clippeth hire ful ofte**   embraced her often.
1203 And he led her home to his palace.

The Merchant's Epilogue

The Host expresses some shock at the tale he has just heard, and calls on God to preserve them from a wife such as the one the Merchant has just described. He knows what tricks women can get up to and how they are always deceiving men. His own wife is a great gossip and nags him a good deal, and he regrets marrying her. He is unwilling to say more, though, as he believes there are people in the party who might tell her what he has said.

1207 **Goddes mercy**   may God help us.
1208 I pray to God to preserve me from such a wife.
1209 **sleightes and subtilitees**   tricks and cunning.
1211 **sely**   innocent, simple.
1212 And they will always deviate from the truth.

1215 **povre**   poor.

1216 **But**   except

  labbyng shrewe   gossiping and ill-tempered woman.

1218 **Therof no fors**   it doesn't matter.

1219 But do you know what? I will tell you this in secret.

1220 I'm very sorry that I'm tied to her.

1221 **and**   if.

  rekenen   count.

1222 **ywis I were to nyce**   I would be foolish.

1224 **somme of this meynee**   someone in this company. The
  implication is that he is thinking of the Wife of Bath here.

1226 Since women know how to speak out about such matters.

1227–8 **And eek... tellen al**   and also I'm not clever enough to tell you
  all.

Interpretations

In the opening section of this book we examined the setting and overall context of *The Merchant's Prologue and Tale*. In this section we will discuss in more detail the key elements that you will need to consider in preparing for examination questions on the text.

Exactly what kind of text Chaucer presents us with here will be discussed in the opening section. We will then go on to look at the techniques Chaucer uses to present his characters, the ways in which he uses language to achieve his effects, and the themes and ideas explored through the text.

Throughout this section there are a number of activities for you to think about, followed by discussions of some of the ideas that they raise. The section concludes with a consideration of critical views, which present a variety of ways of looking at the text.

Narrative voice

In studying any of the *Canterbury Tales* you should think carefully about the narrative voice through which the tale is told. Although *The Merchant's Tale* is presented as if it is being told by the Merchant himself, the narrative voice behind the whole tale is that of Chaucer. Sometimes the comments and ideas being put forward might be those of Chaucer, or he might be presenting them as the views of the Merchant in order to reveal certain things about that character. Another narrative layer is provided by the characters the Merchant is describing. Sometimes Chaucer gives them a voice through direct speech, and they provide another way of presenting ideas that the audience may agree with, disagree with, or laugh at. The irony that forms an important element in the tale often works through this awareness of narrative voice.

Genre

The presentation of *The Merchant's Tale* draws very much on the tradition of the 'fabliau', which had originated in France and had become a very popular form in England by the fourteenth century. Essentially, fabliaux were short, comic narrative tales, usually with ribald and bawdy elements and colourful, lively characters. Very often this kind of tale involves the playing of some kind of trick on one of the characters, and the tricksters often end by being tricked themselves or having the trick backfire on them.

Chaucer adapted this form as the basis of several of his tales, often using the comedy to focus on aspects of human life and behaviour, or on topics such as marriage, the treatment of women, and religion. This was an ideal form through which Chaucer could entertain his audience and at the same time touch upon serious issues and ideas. *The Miller's Tale* is perhaps the best-known example of Chaucer's use of the fabliau, but several other tales, including *The Reeve's Tale* and *The Summoner's Tale*, make use of it too.

In *The Merchant's Tale*, however, Chaucer uses the fabliau form in a very different way from *The Miller's Tale*. In *The Miller's Tale* the characters are from the lower orders of society and much of the humour relies on bawdy and obscene actions and the use of crude language. *The Merchant's Tale* presents its comedy in a more refined way, although in both tales the characters are driven by sexual motives. However, *The Merchant's Tale* also differs in another significant way: in addition to the comic tale, there are also some extended passages discussing the topic of marriage, the nature of women, and relationships between the sexes. These sections create a completely different tone from that of the fabliau-like story, and use a wide range of *auctoritees* (references and classical sources) to support the various points they make. Chaucer weaves these differing elements into a single story, using them to raise many questions and ambiguities about the themes he explores.

The tale, then, is in part a fabliau, partly a court romance focusing on Damyan's infatuation with May, and partly a sermon on women and marriage.

Activity

List the ways in which Chaucer uses the fabliau form in *The Merchant's Tale*.

Discussion

Some of the fabliau features include the following.
- The central theme of the story is the cuckolded husband (as in *The Miller's Tale*), but here the characters are from the world of the aristocracy, the elderly January being a prosperous knight.
- January's young wife, May, and her would-be lover, January's squire and servant Damyan, are attracted to each other, although January is completely unaware of this.
- They play a trick on him so that they can have sex with each other without him realizing it.
- There is much discussion of sexual activity and especially his own sexual prowess by January. The old knight's lust for the young May, May's eagerness to arrange a liaison with Damyan, and the young squire's equally powerful urge to possess her are the key drivers of the plot.
- There is some description of love-making, such as the account of Damyan's liaison with May in the tree, but unlike some fabliaux there is no use of crude or bawdy language.
- The intervention of Pluto and Proserpina – causing the failure of Damyan and May's trick as January's sight is restored, and May's clever escape from his accusations of infidelity – creates a comic ending in keeping with the fabliau form.

Characterization

The Merchant

We are given a brief initial impression of the Merchant in Chaucer's portrait of him in the *General Prologue*. This impression is developed further by what the Merchant has to say, first in the Prologue to his tale and then in the tale itself. Although in the tale he is primarily concerned with telling his story, we also learn about him and his attitudes, both from the kind of tale he tells and the way he tells it.

Activity

Look at the description of the Merchant in the *General Prologue* (page 15). Make a list of the things you learn about the Merchant from this description.

Discussion

Chaucer's description here suggests that the Merchant is a wealthy cloth trader. You might have noted some of the following points.

- He wears a *forked berd* – beards of this kind were very fashionable at this time.
- His clothing is of *mottelee*, a multi-coloured cloth, again fashionable at this time.
- The description *hye on horse he sat* suggests a proud, even arrogant, figure.
- The elegant *bever hat* from Flanders gives a sense of a link with the Continent.
- His riding boots with their elegant fastenings add further to the sense of a wealthy, fashionable merchant.
- He is described as speaking seriously, perhaps even pompously, and there is a little ambiguity in Chaucer's comment that he was always talking about the profits he made. It could suggest an element of boasting and that he always turned the conversation around to the topic of making money.
- The references to Middelburgh in Holland and Orwell in Suffolk confirm the international nature of the Merchant's business.
- His concern about piracy and the possible disruption this could cause to trade emphasizes where his priorities lie.
- His involvement in currency exchange reflects the financially sophisticated world he operates in. Some have suggested that there is a hint of dubious dealings here.
- The final lines of Chaucer's portrait confirm that the Merchant was in debt, but was clever enough to make sure that no one knew this. Obviously, if it becomes known that a businessman is

in debt this could have a negative effect on the confidence of his potential customers or suppliers.

Activity

How does the Merchant's Prologue prepare his audience for his tale?

Discussion

The Merchant opens his Prologue by paraphrasing the closing words of the Clerk, who had concluded his tale with the words *And lat hym care, and wepe, and wrynge, and waille!* The Clerk had told a tale about the marriage of a knight, a topic that the Merchant revisits in his own tale. Picking up on the Clerk's words, the Merchant comments that his own married life has taught him enough about worry and weeping and wailing night and day, explaining that he has the worst wife there could be. He knows too that many more have suffered as he has suffered.

He tells the audience that he cannot describe how cruel his wife is, but she is an absolute shrew. He draws a comparison between the patient wife, Griselda, in the Clerk's tale, and the boundless cruelty of his own wife, and wishes that he had never become trapped by

Griselda, patiently bearing the loss of her child, as told in *The Clerk's Tale*

93

marriage. He tells the audience that he has been married only two months, and comments that he now sees that for most men marriage is full of worry and suffering. The Host replies that as he knows so much about marriage, he should tell them more. The Merchant agrees to pursue the topic but refuses to tell them any more about his own marriage.

In linking the *Merchant's Prologue* directly to *The Clerk's Tale* which immediately precedes it, Chaucer signals the continuing exploration of the theme of marriage started by the Wife of Bath and continued by the Clerk. The Merchant's ready agreement to the Host's request to tell them more about marriage, even though he refuses to say any more about his own experiences, suggests that his view of marriage will be a negative one.

The tale itself consists of two key strands. First there is the story itself involving January, his desire to marry, his search for a bride and the consequences of his marriage. Secondly, there is the discussion about women and marriage contributed to by the Merchant, Placebo and Justinus, and Pluto and Proserpina, all of whose discussions relate to the central theme of the story.

January

Of the various characters in the tale, January is of central importance and is the most developed. He has a dual role. First, he has the comic role of the elderly cuckolded husband, typical of a fabliau. More than this, however, he also contributes to the discussion of marriage that runs through the tale. His contribution in this respect can be seen in the amount of dialogue Chaucer gives him.

Names are of significance, too. 'January' suggests winter and the year's end, as opposed to spring suggested by the name 'May', with its connotations of the freshness and vitality of young life.

Activity

Look at the opening of the tale (lines 33–64). What do you notice about the Merchant's presentation of January here, bearing in mind what happens in the tale?

Discussion

You might have noted the following points.

- The Merchant (as narrator) calls the knight *worthy*. Do you think this an appropriate description in the light of what we learn later?
- Up to this point, January has led a lecherous life following his *bodily delyt / On wommen, ther as was his appetyt* (37–38).
- Now that he has turned 60, January has decided to marry, but his reasons for doing so appear ambiguous: *Were it for hoolynesse or for dotage* (41) – either out of piety or senility. This ambiguity is emphasized further by the narrator's own comment, *I kan nat seye*.
- Bearing in mind the Merchant's earlier comments about marriage, his description of January's view of marriage is particularly ironic:

Preyinge oure Lord to graunten him that he
Mighte ones knowe of thilke blisful lyf
That is bitwixe an housbonde and his wyf

(lines 46–48)

- The further comment *Thanne is a wyf the fruyt of his tresor* (58) creates images of both life and fruitfulness as well as material wealth, again contributing an element of ambiguity to January's attitude.
- The image of the paradise of the Garden of Eden and the binding together of man and woman by God is used here to create a sense of a blissful happiness to be found in marriage. However, the use of this image also carries with it connotations of the fall from grace of Adam and Eve.
- Another reason given by January for wanting to marry is to produce an heir – although this does seem to be very much a secondary consideration for him.

Later in the tale we learn about January's attempts to find a suitable bride, which show other sides to his character.

Activity

Look at lines 181–210. What initial steps does January take to find a bride, and what do his criteria for choosing the ideal bride tell you about him?

Discussion

He thinks about the *lusty lyf* he has led and the *vertuous quyete* that awaits him in *mariage hony-sweete* (183–184), and he sends for his friends to tell them of his decision to marry. The first reason he gives them for his decision is that he intends to marry because he is getting old and close to dying. It has often been noted, though, that if this was really the case it might have been more appropriate for him to turn towards a more spiritual life. After the lifestyle he has told us he has led to this point, his soul may well be in need of some preparation for heaven.

Instead, though, he wants to find a young bride and, having enlisted his friends' help he is quite specific about his requirements. There is no way that he will entertain the idea of an older wife – despite the fact he is 60, he considers any woman approaching 30 to be old, and he is set on finding a bride no older than 20.

Note January's use of animal imagery in describing how he sees the difference between young and old:

'Oold fissh and yong flessh wolde I have fayn.
Bet is,' quod he, 'a pyk than a pykerel,
And bet than old boef is the tendre veel.'

(lines 206–208)

His use here of imagery connected to animals and to meat that can be consumed gives a sense of appetite, his sexual appetite. He prefers mature fish and young flesh, and in this sense he is the pike, an aggressive and voracious fish, and the young woman is the tender veal, ready to be 'caught' to feed his sexual appetite. Older women, of 30 or more, are compared to dried beanstalks and rough fodder, and as such are unproductive and undesirable to him.

January goes on to talk about the disadvantages of older women and the advantages of younger ones.

Activity

What does he have to say about old widows, young women and marriage in lines 211–243?

Discussion

He talks of the craftiness of old widows, who have learned cunning ways to manipulate their husbands. Many critics have commented that this seems to be a reference, by Chaucer, via the Merchant and January, to the Wife of Bath, who successfully gets the better of several old husbands.

He uses the image of *warm wex* (218) to describe young girls as quite a different proposition: they are malleable and can be moulded to suit his will and desire. If he were unfortunate enough to marry an older woman he would not find her attractive and so he would be driven to commit adultery, and therefore go to hell when he died. Also, he would not be able to have children with an older wife. His desire for an heir seems apparent through his choice of imagery when he says that he would rather be eaten by hounds than have his property inherited by strangers.

He feels that if a man cannot live a celibate life then he should take a wife out of religious devotion, in order to have children who are legitimate in the eyes of God and to turn away from lechery. Ironically, it has taken 60 years for January to arrive at this view. Continuing in this vein, January says he feels that husband and wife should help each other and live a life of holy chastity, like brother and sister.

Commenting on his own advanced years, January tells them the whiteness of his hair is like the blossom of the tree that allows its fruit to form. He assures them that although his hair may be white, his heart and limbs are as green and as full of life as the evergreen laurel tree (which contradicts his earlier statement that one of his reason for marrying is that he is almost on his *pittes brynke*, 189).

January's comments here, of course, are all full of contradictions. Does he want to marry because he is getting old, and as death approaches he wants to make sure his soul is cleansed ready for an easy passage to heaven? In his twilight years, does he want the tranquil life provided by the companionship of a faithful wife? Is he concerned that he has no heir to inherit his wealth and property? Or does he want to carry on his lecherous ways within the sanctity of marriage? Certainly he provides us with a host of reasons for his decision, many of which seem ambiguous and contradictory. However, from his later behaviour, it is easy to see where a good deal of his motivation comes from.

Eventually January finds a suitable bride in the young and very attractive May, and he immediately begins to fantasize about her:

> And whan that he was in his bed ybroght,
> He purtreyed in his herte and in his thoght
> Hir fresshe beautee and hir age tendre,
> Hir myddel smal, hire armes longe and sklendre,
> Hir wise governaunce, hir gentillesse,
> Hir wommanly berynge, and hire sadnesse.

(lines 387–392)

It is clear here that January's thoughts are very much on May's physical attributes, but it is worth noting that her attractiveness to him seems to go beyond the purely physical. He speaks also of her wise and sensible demeanour and her *gentillesse*, nobility of character (despite the fact that she is not of noble birth). He also admires her *wommanly berynge* and serious manner. She is, in his mind at least, his ideal wife.

January intends to waste no time and wants the wedding arrangements made quickly. Very soon the marriage takes place. However, as the wedding feast begins to draw to a close, January's focus on May begins to change a little as he thinks about the night to come.

Activity

Look at lines 538–555. What do you notice about the language used to describe January's thoughts and feelings here?

Discussion

You might have noticed the line *But in his herte he gan hire to manace*, which has disturbing connotations of violence. His fantasy of restraining her hard in his arms reinforces this impression. This sense of taking her by force is strengthened further by the use of the simile drawn from the story of Paris abducting Helen of Troy, in Greek mythology. The violence of his passionate feelings, though, is then softened slightly by feelings of pity that he must offend her, and he prays to God that she can endure his powerful sexual desires. Note the use of the words *sharp and keene* here, with connotations of a knife, and consider what this reveals about January's own opinion of his sexual prowess.

Driven by his sexual desire for May, January encourages his guests to leave and he retires to bed with his new bride at last.

Activity

What impression does Chaucer create of January when he finally takes May to bed, and how does May respond to his love-making?

Discussion

Chaucer concentrates on the unpleasant and unsavoury aspects of January here – with his frequent kisses May feels the *thikke brustles of his berd unsofte* (612) – an experience made to seem all the more unpleasant by the simile comparing this to the skin of a dogfish, suggesting a sandpaper-like feel to January's face. Another simile, *sharp as brere*, further emphasizes this unpleasantness. The effect on May is made even more clear by the contrast of his scratchy face against May's tender cheek.

His apology in advance for the violence of his love-making and his comparison of himself to a workman going about his task indicate his belief that he is skilled at love-making and that it is likely to go on for some considerable time:

> Ther nys no werkman, whatsoevere he be,
> That may bothe werke wel and hastily;
> This wol be doon at leyser parfitly.

(lines 620–622)

99

He continues with his 'labours' until dawn, when he takes some bread dipped in wine and then begins to sing. The description here continues to make January sound unpleasant – full of lechery, as frisky as a colt, full of passion and chattering like a magpie. The slack skin of January's neck, shaking as he sings (or, more accurately, croaks), causes the Merchant to ponder on what May *thoughte in hir herte*, and he comments to his audience that she does not think much of it:

> Whan she hym saugh up sittynge in his sherte,
> In his nyght-cappe, and with his nekke lene;
> She preyseth nat his pleyyng worth a bene.

(lines 640–642)

A print showing January and May made in 1782 – notice the depiction of the keys

May

In the tale, May is far less developed as a character than January, and in some ways simply performs the role of the young, attractive wife with a jealous old husband. When she falls for the charms of an attractive young man and the couple use trickery to create the opportunity to cuckold the old husband, the plot-line follows the popular fabliau form.

With May, we are not given the same sense of a developed character as we get with January, but there are moments in the tale where Chaucer does give us some sense of her personality. The first of these occasions is the comment about May's thoughts on January's singing at the end of their wedding night, as quoted above.

Activity

Make a list of other examples where Chaucer gives the audience some sense of May as a character.

Discussion

Once May is aware of Damyan's feelings for her and she realizes that she desires him too, she takes control and tells him what to do. Chaucer presents her thoughts to the audience directly:

> 'Certeyn,' thoghte she, 'whom that this thyng displese
> I rekke noght, for heere I hym assure
> To love hym best of any creature,
> Though he namoore hadde than his sherte.'

(lines 770–773)

When she writes the letter telling him she will sleep with him as soon as possible, and places it under his pillow, it is clear that May is now driving the action of the plot. It also seems clear that, despite the Merchant's comment earlier that she is acting out of pity (an unusually charitable view bearing in mind his negative opinion of wives), her real motivating factor is lust. She and Damyan are alike in their desires.

It is May who makes an impression of the key in wax – a vital part of the plan – to allow Damyan access to the locked garden. The re-appearance of the idea of moulding wax has often been noted here. Earlier in the tale (see page 97 above), the image was used in describing January's desire to mould a young woman like warm wax into his ideal wife. Ironically, wax is being moulded here to allow Damyan into January's 'paradise' and to take from him this ideal wife.

Throughout the whole of the execution of the plot it is May who orchestrates the action. She persuades January to take her to the garden. She tells Damyan to hide himself there. She signals to him to climb the tree. Whether or not Chaucer means us to believe that May is really pregnant does not matter, but again she drives the plot by persuading the blind January to hug the tree so she can climb on his back to reach her lover. This ridiculous situation is, of course, a device essential to the plot. The irony of May invoking the name of *hir... that is of hevene queene* here to add weight to her words (1122) is clear.

Finally, the plot needs a resolution, and May has a notably quick-witted response to January's accusations when, sight restored, he sees what is going on. She persuades him that he has misread the situation, and delivers the final blow by making January appear in the wrong:

> 'Ye maze, maze, goode sire,' quod she;
> 'This thank have I for I have maad yow see.
> Allas,' quod she, 'that evere I was so kynde!'
>
> (lines 1175–1177)

Damyan

There is little development of character in the presentation of Damyan, nor, in terms of the plot, does there need to be. In the tale he is the conventional courtly lover and the means by which the foolish old husband is cuckolded.

Activity

How are these two roles of Damyan presented in the tale, and what is the effect?

Discussion

First, as the courtly lover, Damyan is the young squire who falls in love with May at first sight and becomes so love-sick he has to take to his bed, although he recovers instantly once he knows his love is reciprocated. His second role, equally stereotypical, is to provide the means by which the foolish old husband is cuckolded. Within the fabliau framework of the tale, no real development of his character is required and he is barely given a voice, speaking only two lines throughout. We hear him speak only when he gives his secret letter to May and begs her:

> 'Mercy! And that ye nat discovere me,
> For I am deed if that this thyng be kyd.'

(lines 730–731)

There is very little interaction between Damyan and May apart, of course, from the sexual activity in the pear tree, which is a stock situation and forms a key part of the climax of the tale. There is also no interaction or dialogue between him and his master, January. The effect of this is to allow the audience's attention to be focused fully and without distraction on January and May.

Placebo and Justinus

Placebo and Justinus are very much symbolic characters in the tale and, like the stock characters we have examined so far, they perform a specific function within the narrative.

Activity

Look at the section of the tale in which Placebo and Justinus appear (lines 266–476). How do they, in their different ways, contribute to the discussions about January's marriage plans?

Discussion

Placebo and Justinus act in the role of counsellors to January, advising him on his plan to marry. However, they are contrasted in the stance they take on this. As explained in the Notes, in Latin the word 'placebo' means 'I will please', and this is ideally suited to Placebo's approach to offering advice. In his opening words he flatters January by telling him that he is so full of wisdom he has no need to ask advice from anyone. Placebo goes on to give his judgement, which is quite simple: *I holde youre owene conseil is the beste* (line 278). In other words, do not rely on the advice of others but on your own feelings about what is best. He thus agrees with January that it is a good idea for an old man to marry a young wife.

Justinus's name also derives from Latin, and means 'fair', 'righteous' and 'just', thereby suggesting that he is likely to give honest and considered opinions. He disagrees with Placebo's view and cites Seneca to support his opinion that:

> a man oghte hym right wel avyse
> To whom he yeveth his lond or his catel.
> And syn I oghte avyse me right wel
> To whom I yeve my good awey fro me,
> Wel muchel moore I oghte avysed be
> To whom I yeve my body for alwey.

(lines 312–317)

He goes on to list the questions that need to be asked in establishing the virtues or vices of a potential bride. A preponderance of negative views shapes his questions, however, suggesting that his focus is on looking for vices rather than appreciating virtues. He does add that the advice he is offering January is based very much on his own experience. January, though, is dismissive of Justinus's view and that of Seneca too, whom Justinus cites in support of his opinion. Justinus, realizing that January's mind is made up, stops arguing his case and adopts a slightly scathing tone, making a joke out of January's worries about getting to heaven:

> Justinus, which that hated his folye,
> Answerde anon right in his japerye

(lines 443–444)

Justinus abandons any further attempts to advise January, seeing that his mind is made up and all contrary advice ignored, and he takes his leave.

Pluto and Proserpina

The last two characters in the tale are Pluto and Proserpina, who are figures from Greek mythology. According to the myth, Pluto, the god of the Underworld, came across Proserpina when he found her gathering flowers in the valley of Enna in Sicily. He was immediately captivated by her beauty and, forcing her into his chariot, carried her away to the Underworld and made her his queen. In the tale, these two characters are presented as the King and Queen of Fairyland who visit the mortal world from time to time and observe the activities of human beings.

Activity

In what ways do Pluto and Proserpina perform an important role in the tale?

Discussion

Pluto and Proserpina have two main functions in the development of the plot. First, they have a purely practical function in enabling the fantastic events at the conclusion of the play to take place. The restoration of January's sight comes about through Pluto's magic, while May's incredible excuse for what is going on is inspired by Proserpina. In this sense, these characters are devices that move the action of the plot towards its conclusion through their magical powers.

However, they do have another function in the contribution they make to the central theme of the tale, the debate about marriage and relationships between men and women. In the argument that takes place between them, Pluto cites evidence, in much the same way as the Merchant and Justinus did earlier, to support the idea that women are unreliable. Proserpina angrily rejects his views, and their heated argument on relations between men and women adds an important dimension to the overall debate.

Themes

The marriage debate

The central theme of *The Merchant's Tale* is marriage, and it is one of a group of tales linked by their exploration of this theme. This group consists of *The Wife of Bath's Prologue and Tale*, *The Merchant's Prologue and Tale*, *The Squire's Tale* and *The Franklin's Prologue and Tale*. It is clear from what the Merchant has to say in his Prologue that his tale will be focused on the subject of marriage, and every part of the tale contributes in some way to the exploration of this topic.

The tale takes its starting point from the fact that January decides, after a life of lechery, that at the age of 60 it is time for him to find a suitable wife and settle down:

> 'Noon oother lyf,' seyde he, 'is worth a bene,
> For wedlok is so esy and so clene,
> That in this world it is a paradys.'
>
> (lines 51–53)

Immediately after he has begun his tale, though, and introduced January and his intention to marry, there is an interruption as the Merchant describes views on the benefits and drawbacks of marriage. There is some debate about who these opinions belong to, January or the Merchant, although generally they are attributed to the Merchant.

Activity

What views about marriage does the Merchant put forward in lines 55–180?

Discussion

The first set of views are expressed in lines 55–80. It is a *glorious thyng* for a man to take a wife, particularly if the man is old and white-haired. He should take a *yong wyf and a feir* who can provide him

Themes

with an heir and allow him to live a life of joy and contentment. Young bachelors often sigh and mope when they encounter problems in love and lack security and maturity. A married man, on the other hand, achieves a state of bliss, although interestingly he tells of living *a lyf blisful and ordinaat / Under this yok of mariage ybounde* (lines 72–73). This metaphor of marriage as a 'yoke' under which the husband is bowed may indicate an ironic comment on the Merchant's own experience of married life.

He then comments on the love and care that a wife tirelessly bestows on her husband, even if he lies bedridden until death.

In lines 81–106, the narrator rejects the view of Theophrastus, a classical writer who wrote on the subject of marriage and held that wives were only interested in getting their hands on their husbands' money. Theophrastus's view was that a faithful servant would show more care, diligence and loyalty and that a man's possessions and money would be safer with them than with a wife. In addition to this, Theophrastus warned that a man who takes a wife is very likely to be cuckolded. The Merchant concludes his attack on Theophrastus

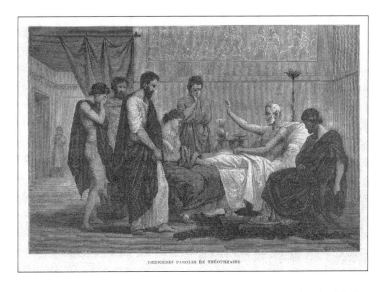

A print depicting the Greek philosopher Theophrastus on his deathbed

in this way:

> This sentence, and an hundred thynges worse,
> Writeth this man, ther God his bones corse!
> But take no kep of al swich vanytee;
> Deffie Theofraste, and herke me.

(lines 95–98)

In opposition to Theophrastus's view, according to the Merchant a wife is a gift from God, surpassing all other kinds of gifts because the pleasures and benefits those gifts offer are purely a matter of Fortune and will pass like a shadow on a wall.

In lines 107–180, the narrator affirms that marriage is a momentous sacrament and he views anyone who does not possess a wife as cursed and destined to live in loneliness and sorrow. He cites the Bible's creation story to support this, and recalls how Eve was created to be Adam's helper and the source of his earthly pleasure and enjoyment. The narrator continues to extol the virtues of having a wife and the benefits wives bring, and says that a married man should give thanks to God all his life for providing him with a wife. He cites further evidence from the Bible to support his argument, giving examples of wives from the Old Testament who showed great resourcefulness. However, it is worth noting here the irony attached to the cases he chooses:

- the example of Jacob involves Rebecca, who wants her younger son Jacob to inherit his father's wealth and achieves this by tricking her elderly and blind husband, Isaac, into thinking that Jacob is their elder son, Esau
- in the next example, Judith saves the Israelites by seducing Holofernes, the general of the enemy Assyrian army threatening to destroy them; having seduced him she waits until he falls into a drunken sleep and then cuts off his head with a knife
- Abigail is the wife of Nabal who has angered King David; she pleads with David not to punish her husband and David is so impressed with her beauty, intelligence and political shrewdness that he marries her when Nabal dies shortly afterwards
- Esther also saves her people, like Judith, by an act of betrayal: Esther is the Jewish queen married to the Persian King Ahasuerus. She persuades her husband to spare Mordecai, a Jew who refuses

to bow to a Persian nobleman, Haman. However, through Esther, Haman is hanged as a traitor and Mordecai appointed first minister to the king.

These examples of female virtue have one thing in common – they all achieved their ends by betraying a man who had placed some trust in them. These add to the strongly ironical sense of this diversion from the story, and perhaps cast a slightly different light on the tale overall.

As the story continues we learn more about January's ideas on marriage.

Activity

What does January's attitude to marriage seem to be?

Discussion

January gives several reasons for wishing to marry.
- He is getting old and feels that it is time for him to marry for, despite his past loose living, he now recognizes marriage as being a blissful and desirable state. He speaks of the spiritual state of husband and wife living within the *hooly boond* of God (49), *That in this world it is a paradys* (53).
- He insists that he will only marry a girl who is 20 or younger, suggesting perhaps that his old lecherous inclinations have not entirely been converted into an interest in a more spiritual kind of relationship between man and woman.
- Older women, especially widows, are too clever at manipulating and managing their husbands, whereas he will be able to mould a young woman into the kind of wife he wants.
- A young wife will also be able to provide him with children, and he wants an heir to inherit his property. Marriage to an older woman would probably lead him to commit adultery in order to produce an heir, and that would send him to hell when he dies.

You might notice in January's reasons some contradictory ideas. On the one hand he claims he wants to marry for religious reasons, in order to avoid sin, and on the other hand he wants a woman to fulfil his lustful desires, a motive that we see confirmed as the tale progresses. These contradictions built into the central character are a key element in the development of Chaucer's ideas in the tale, and raise various questions.

The two friends that January calls upon to give him advice on his plan to marry, Placebo and Justinus, also present conflicting ideas.

Activity

Look at the section of the tale where Placebo and Justinus offer their views (lines 266–364). What advice does January receive from each of them?

Discussion

Placebo adopts the position of a flatterer who praises January's wisdom and tells him he does not need to rely on the advice of others. He agrees with January that it is an excellent idea for an older man to marry a young woman. Justinus, though, disagrees with this view and with January's plans, and urges him to consider the matter very carefully. Giving away his property is a serious matter and marriage needs to be given very careful thought. Justinus adds weight to his view by telling January that he speaks from experience:

> For, God it woot, I have wept many a teere
> Ful pryvely, syn I have had a wyf.
> Preyse whoso wole a wedded mannes lyf,
> Certein I fynde in it but cost and care
> And observances, of alle blisses bare.

(lines 332–336)

However, January does not want to hear such advice and much prefers the flattery of Placebo, who basically agrees with everything January says. January is blind to the warnings of Justinus, just as he later becomes physically blind to the situation between May and Damyan. Justinus's words are dismissed out of hand:

'Wel', quod this Januarie, 'and hastow ysayd?
Straw for thy Senek, and for thy proverbes!
I counte nat a panyer ful of herbes
Of scole-termes.'

(lines 354–357)

Placebo, of course, agrees and curses anyone who stands in the way of January's marriage.

The antagonism between men and women, as seen through the writings of scholars such as Theophrastus commented on by the Merchant at the beginning of his tale, form the basis of Justinus's arguments against January's plan. These arguments are paralleled by the argument between Pluto and Proserpina towards the end of the tale.

Activity

What begins the argument between Pluto and Proserpina, and how does it develop (lines 1025–1107)?

Discussion

Pluto begins with an attack on treacherous wives, and this starts an argument between him and Proserpina. Pluto claims he could find a million tales of the *tresons whiche that wommen doon to man* (1027). He cites evidence from the Bible to support his view of the unreliability of women, and he defends January, saying that he will restore the old man's sight.

Proserpina responds by telling him that in return she will give May, and every accused woman after her, the ability to convince her husband of her innocence. Angry at her husband's attack on women, Proserpina goes on to reject the authorities he has cited to support his argument, claiming that Pluto's argument is biased and his evidence selective.

In the end Pluto gives in, but tells Proserpina that he will still give January back his sight, and she maintains that she will keep her promise of enabling May to persuade January of her innocence.

Anti-feminism

The society of medieval England was a very male-dominated one in which women had very little power and the laws governing what they could and could not do, set by men, greatly limited their freedom. There is a strong anti-feminist element in a good deal of the literature of the Middle Ages, often stemming from the association of women with Eve, who according to the Bible caused the Fall of Man. The writings of St Jerome had a significant influence in shaping the medieval view of women. In her Prologue, Chaucer's Wife of Bath points to the existence of various anti-feminist texts, specifically St Jerome's treatise *Adversus Jovinianum*, in which he affirms his view that a celibate life is far superior to married life. He argues against the Jovinian view that a virgin is no better than a wife in the sight of God, claiming virginity is much superior, as virginity is the natural state while marriage is the result of the Fall.

It could be argued that *The Merchant's Tale* presents both a pro-feminist and an anti-feminist stance.

The Wife of Bath, from the Ellesmere manuscript

Activity

What anti-feminist views does the tale present?

Discussion

The comments of the Merchant in his Prologue reveal his regret at ever having married. He tells his audience that his wife is the worst wife there could be, and the strength of his feelings is expressed through extreme comments such as:

> For thogh the feend to hire ycoupled were,
> She wolde hym overmacche, I dar wel swere.

(lines 7–8)

In fact, he is so moved at the very thought of the suffering she has put him through that he cannot even bear to talk about it further.

If it is accepted that the lines on marriage at the beginning of the tale are in the voice of the Merchant, then it is possible to see sharp irony in this extended praise of the virtues of marriage. According to this view, the Merchant's words are delivered very much tongue-in-cheek, the joke being made all the more relevant because these are exactly the views that January believes and wants to hear.

The advice offered to January by Justinus is, like the Merchant's views, apparently based on his personal experiences. His comments reveal an extreme anti-feminist viewpoint in his presentation of the vices in a woman as a potential wife that January should be aware of. It is notable that the vices he warns about far outweigh any potential virtues to be found in women; he focuses on drunkenness, arrogance, shrewishness and extravagance. He comments too on what he sees as women's tendency to infidelity, and says that:

> The yongeste man that is in al this route
> Is bisy ynough to bryngen it aboute
> To han his wyf allone.

(lines 347–349)

To some extent, however, these anti-feminist views are counterbalanced in the tale.

Activity

What positive views of women do you find in the tale?

Discussion

Some writers have pointed to the presentation of May as being positive in that it shows her as a strong female character. She is clearly aware of the situation she is entering into with January, and does not appear intimidated by January's boasts of his sexual prowess. In fact, at the end of their wedding night – which concludes with January bursting into song – she seems completely unimpressed. Far from being a meek, obedient wife she takes control of events, planning her meeting with Damyan and instructing him what to do. She also controls January quite easily, and when it seems that she will be found out she quick-wittedly manages to talk her way out of trouble (with the aid of Proserpina's powers).

Proserpina also offers a positive female model in countering the arguments of her husband Pluto who, in his defence of the betrayed January, accuses women of being unreliable. Proserpina's vehement defence of women and her criticism of his citing of Solomon to support his points eventually forces Pluto to give in. This represents the dominance of her argument over the anti-feminist views presented by Pluto.

Language and style

Verse form

Like most of Chaucer's *Canterbury Tales*, the Merchant's Prologue and tale are written in iambic pentameter. This means that each line consists of five metrical feet (or iambs), each made up of an unstressed and a stressed syllable. Each line, therefore contains ten syllables, as you can see if you analyse the following passage, sounding out all the syllables:

> 'Ne take no wyf,' quod he, 'for housbondrye,
> As for to spare in houshold thy dispence.

> A trewe servant dooth moore diligence
> Thy good to kepe than thyn owene wyf,
> For she wol clayme half part al hir lyf.'
>
> (lines 84–88)

This verse pattern is noted for using a rhythm very close to the rhythms of normal speech, and so allows Chaucer to create a natural tone to his verse. However, he does not adhere strictly to iambic pentameter, but adapts it and uses it flexibly to suit his purpose. He also uses rhyming couplets, which add a further sense of rhythm and movement to the lines.

A number of stylistic elements blend together to create the overall effect of the tale. It combines the comic effects of the fabliau with extended passages of serious debate on the topic of women and marriage, drawing on examples from the Bible and classical scholars. The kind of language Chaucer uses in the tale reflects this. For example, courtly language is used to present Damyan in places, but this sometimes switches to a more forthright style such as that used to describe his love-making to May in the pear tree. The effect of these switches in both tone and style is to help suggest the nature of his human urges underneath the courtly pose.

There are also some passages of moralizing, drawing on the support of learned *auctoritees*. These can be seen in the comments of Placebo and Justinus and the argument between Pluto and Proserpina, and also in the comments of the Merchant at the beginning of the tale. Some passages – and the overall plot – create the comic effect of the typical fabliau, although the tale is more refined than *The Miller's Tale* and lacks the crude actions, focus on bodily functions, and obscene language to be found in that story. However, the 'moralizing' passages take the form beyond that of the pure fabliau, and the more serious discussion gives it an added dimension and moral weight. Within this broad form, various elements combine to create Chaucer's overall effects. One aspect of this is his use of imagery.

Imagery

Chaucer often uses recurring imagery, which creates a series of motifs that connect throughout the tale.

Activity

Identify some key images that you have noted in the tale and explore the effects they create.

Discussion

Imagery associated with food and drink is used at various points in the tale. For example, in discussing his desire to marry a young woman, January uses imagery associated with fish and flesh. He prefers mature fish and young meat, saying that tender veal is better than old beef. Clearly a young woman is 'young meat' and 'tender veal' to January.

Older women, however, are described as *bene-straw and greet forage* (210) – dried-up stalks of the crop from which the wholesome grain has been extracted, and course fodder given to animals as food.

Later the word *tendre* is used again to describe May on her wedding night, and this time it is contrasted against the sharpness of January's sexual desire, which is described through rather disturbing knife imagery:

> O tendre creature,
> Now wolde God ye myghte wel endure
> Al my corage, it is so sharp and keene!
>
> (lines 545–547)

This produces the double effect of first creating a threatening, aggressive image – especially when coupled with January's concern about whether May will survive the violence of his passionate love-making – but then defusing any serious connotations through the humour created by the deluded January's idea of his own sexual prowess.

As noted above, the image of warm wax, used to indicate that a young woman is more pliable than an older one and can be moulded and shaped to the will of the husband, reappears later in the tale where May uses wax to make an impression of the key to January's walled garden. The irony here is clear, in that May – likened to wax in being shaped to her husband's will – uses that material as an important tool in the deception and cuckolding of the husband; a wax impression allows the cuckolder to violate January's private 'paradise'.

There are other extended uses of imagery. For example, Chaucer creates a convincing voice for the Merchant as the teller of the tale through his use of mercantile images. In speaking of the benefits of marriage, he describes the gift from God of a wife, comparing her to property:

> A wyf is Goddes yifte verraily;
> Alle othere manere yiftes hardily,
> As londes, rentes, pasture, or commune,
> Or moebles – alle been yiftes of Fortune
> That passen as a shadwe upon a wal.

(lines 99–103)

Similarly, one of Justinus's key points in warning January of the danger of marriage is that a man should be very careful of giving away his goods and property:

> a man oghte hym right wel avyse
> To whom he yeveth his lond or his catel.

(lines 312–313)

Also, January himself refers to May as his 'treasure'. The threat to January's happiness in his self-made paradise is posed, of course, by Damyan, who is intent on taking January's treasure for himself. To add emphasis to the danger he poses he is described through imagery of fire, a fire that starts in the bed:

> O perilous fyr, that in the bedstraw bredeth!
> O famulier foo, that his servyce bedeth!
> O servant traytour, false hoomly hewe,
> Lyk to the naddre in bosom sly untrewe

(lines 571–574)

Damyan is linked with fire in another way too, when he is described as burning up with the fire of love in his passion for May:

> This sike Damyan in Venus fyr

So brenneth that he dyeth for desyr,
For which he putte his lyf in aventure.

(lines 663–665)

Symbols

Symbols form a key part of Chaucer's use of imagery in the tale. The symbolic aspects of some features are highlighted, giving them a significance that takes them beyond their surface meaning.

Activity

Identify three examples and show how Chaucer uses symbols in the tale.

Discussion

1 Names: The names of some of the characters in the tale have a particular symbolic significance. For example, January is an old man and the name has connotations of winter. His description of himself as being *hoor* or white-haired creates an image of the whiteness of a hoar frost. May's name, on the other hand, suggests the life and brightness of springtime and youth. It is noticeable that often the adjective *fresshe* is coupled with her name.

2 The garden and the tree: The Garden of Eden, as a paradise, is an image that holds a symbolic significance throughout the tale. There is an early reference to Adam and the story that God created Eve to give him the gift of a wife. As the plot develops, the image of the garden is interwoven into the tale. The symbolic importance of January's creation of his own 'garden of paradise' is clear here. As in the biblical garden, a corrupting element enters and his wife betrays him. Also as in the biblical story, the tree plays an important role in January's betrayal, although the tree here is a pear tree and not the apple tree associated with the Garden of Eden. It is worth noting too that early in the tale January compares himself to a tree in full blossom before the fruit is formed, in describing his own vitality even though he is old. This image of the tree in blossom is a linking image to the pear tree in fruit, which is significant later in the tale as it is the scene of Damyan and May's liaison.

3 January's blindness: On one level this blindness is a plot device that enables May and Damyan to deceive the foolish old husband. However, it also performs a symbolic function within the tale – January is metaphorically blind from start to finish. For example:

- he is blinded by his sexual desires for a young wife
- he is blind to the risks of taking a young bride
- he ignores the advice of Justinus
- he has a distorted view of himself and is convinced of his prowess at love-making
- even when his sight is restored and he discovers May and Damyan making love in the tree, he is still unable to see the truth because of May's persuasive powers; as the Merchant comments, *For love is blynd alday, and may nat see* (line 386).

Irony

Irony is an important feature of Chaucer's writing generally, and it is certainly central to *The Merchant's Prologue and Tale*. Many critics have pointed to the Merchant's praise of marriage at the beginning of his tale as being one of the most extended passages of irony in literature. He interrupts his tale to give his long, rhetorical exposition on the merits of marriage. However, since this immediately follows his bitter comments on the nature of his own brief marriage, his praise appears highly ironic and prepares the way for the many other ironies that are created in the tale.

Activity

List some other examples of irony you find in the tale.

Discussion

Elements of the tale that are clearly meant to be taken ironically include:

- the Merchant's assertion that January's opening comments are spoken out of wisdom: *Thus seyde this olde knyght, that was so wys* (line 54)
- January's insistence on a religious motivation for marriage – his desire to live in *the vertuous quyete, / That is in mariage hony-*

sweete (lines 183–184) – followed by his insistence that he will not consider a bride over 20 years old
- the biblical references juxtaposed against the sexual motivations of the characters
- January's blindness – he is made physically blind, but with regard to love and marriage he is blind throughout the tale. The irony is compounded as, even after Pluto restores his sight, he still does not really 'see'.

Narrative techniques

Chaucer uses a variety of narrative techniques to create his effects in *The Merchant's Prologue and Tale*.

Activity

Make a list of the narrative techniques that Chaucer uses to create his effects.

Discussion

You might have noted the following.
- The Prologue allows the stage to be set for a tale about marriage. The references to the Merchant's personal, negative experience of marriage creates a sense of anticipation about the kind of tale he will tell.
- There is the repeated device of lengthy discussions of marriage and women, with references to a wide range of authorities to support and illustrate the points being made.
- Astrological references, and references to the calendar, as well as pinpointing the timing of events add a further level of comments upon them. For example, after her wedding night, May – in keeping with tradition – stays in her chamber for a few days, and we are told that:

The moone, that at noon was thilke day
That Januarie hath wedded fresshe May
In two of Tawr, was into Cancre glyden

(lines 673–675)

The astrological reference indicates the time spent by May in the isolation of her room.

Chaucer also creates a sense of fate or destiny influencing events:

Were it by influence or by nature,
Or constellacion, that in swich estaat
The hevene stood that tyme fortunaat
Was for to putte a bille of Venus werkes

(lines 756–759)

Later, just before January is struck blind, we are told how he lived his life happily and spent his days making love to May in his garden.

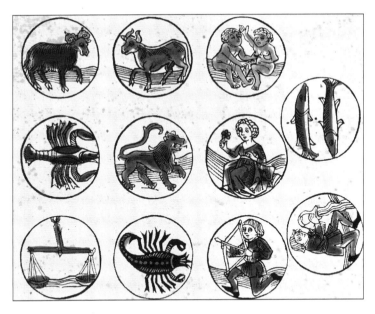

A woodcut representing zodiac signs, dated 1498 – note Taurus (the bull) in the top row, and Cancer (the crab) in the second row

Ominously, though, we are reminded that *worldly joye may nat alwey dure | To Januarie, ne to no creature* (lines 843–844), suggesting to the audience that January's happiness is soon to end.

These lines immediately follow, which link indirectly to Damyan, the threat to January's happiness:

> O sodeyn hap! O thou Fortune unstable!
> Lyk to the scorpion so deceyvable,
> That flaterest with thyn heed whan thou wolt stynge;
> Thy tayl is deeth, thurgh thyn envenymynge.
>
> (lines 845–848)

The scorpion itself is a predator; in astrology, Scorpio rules the genitalia (see the sign in the bottom row of the illustration on the previous page). These lines, following immediately upon those that tell us of the happiness of January's life, suggest to the audience that January's happiness is going to be destroyed by Damyan's sexual advances to May. It is significant that immediately following these lines, January is struck blind.

The unity of Prologue and tale

As mentioned earlier, on the surface the Merchant's Prologue seems out of keeping with the tale he tells. His Prologue outlines briefly his negative experience of married life, but at the beginning of his tale he extols the advantages of marriage and says that a wife will always be helpful and obedient to her husband. However, if taken ironically, this sermon on marriage is completely in keeping with what we know of the Merchant's views, and with many of the attitudes that emerge from the tale itself.

Activity

Make a note of the ways in which you think the Prologue and the tale are linked.

Discussion

The Merchant tells of his unhappiness in marriage and the unpleasantness of his wife; she is the complete opposite of Griselda, the patient wife described by the Clerk in his tale. He appears to use his own negative experience to generalize about how men as a whole find marriage:

> We wedded men lyven in sorwe and care.
> Assaye whoso wole, and he shal fynde
> That I seye sooth
>
> (lines 16–18)

At the beginning of the tale the Merchant praises marriage, but the scholar Theophrastus – whose views he claims to reject – describes marriage as having the very effect on husbands that the Merchant has experienced himself. Theophrastus also warns that wives are very likely to be unfaithful. This view, of course, links directly to the situation in the tale. If the Merchant's comments are taken as being ironic, his apparent praise of women makes sense, as does the kind of tale he tells, where the old husband is fooled through the infidelity of his wife. The women cited in the tale seemingly as role models can again can be regarded as being discussed ironically (see page 109).

The views offered by Justinus provide another link with the Merchant's Prologue. Justinus, like the Merchant, speaks from his own experience and uses authorities to support his ideas, and tells his listeners he has wept many times since he married, and finds marriage nothing *but cost and care* (335). Pluto also talks about the unreliability of women and cites the Bible and other authorities to support his views.

Looked at in this way, the link between the Merchant as narrator and the tale that he tells is clear. However, it is also apparent that behind this narrator is the voice of Chaucer, inviting the audience to adopt a broader view of the tale and the issues it raises – including the nature of women – than the negative and superficial one that appears to be presented.

Critical views

Over the centuries *The Merchant's Tale* has provoked a good deal of debate and disagreement, and critics have looked at it from a variety of viewpoints. One question that was at the centre of early critical debate was the nature of the tale as a fabliau, and often critics focused on the bawdy elements. Other critics saw in the tale a level of insight and sophistication that lifted it beyond a simple fabliau. As we have seen, with its philosophical debate and detailed use of a wide variety of *auctoritees*, the tale offers much more than a bawdy romp.

Context

Historical criticism looks at the text as a work within the context in which it was written. This approach sees the Merchant and his tale as closely linked to the religious beliefs, social structures and socio-economic conditions of the fourteenth century. Critics looking at the text from this point of view argue that we can only really understand the ideas expressed by the characters when we consider this context.

This kind of critical perspective often focuses on the status of women and views on marriage that were current in the England of the Middle Ages. This was an age when it was not unusual for wealthy older men to marry much younger women, and for marriages to be arranged solely for financial or political reasons. This does not discount the undoubtedly lecherous reasons that are part, at least, of January's motivation for marrying but it does, perhaps, cast the age difference between January and his bride into a different light for a modern eye. Many of the religious references and classical allusions, the significance of astrological references and the anti-feminist arguments in the tale, should also be viewed and interpreted in the context of the time of writing, according to this critical approach.

The feminist viewpoint

Feminist and gender criticism has explored a variety of ways of looking at the text, such as its presentation of the traditional medieval view of women, the position of women in a male-dominated society, and the contrast between the sexes. There has been much focus on *The Merchant's Prologue and Tale* in terms of the misogynistic views that are expressed in its criticism of women at various points, but some modern critics have regarded the tale as presenting the foolishness and lechery of men in an equally critical light.

This approach focuses on areas such as May's position – both socially and financially – in relation to the power that January, foolish though he is, holds over her, and questions the significance of the references to Eve and the deceitfulness of women. Some critics develop ideas around May's move from being a passive character, completely subject to the will of January, to a person who takes the initiative and shapes the action of the plot. In January's world, May holds no real power except that which she exerts over him with her body. In her relationship with Damyan, though, it is she who holds the power.

The Merchant and social class

Some critics, such as those adopting a Marxist view of the tale, look at it from the point of view of social class, economics, and power. They note that the mercantile background of the Merchant himself underlies the tale, with repeated references throughout to the language of commerce.

Such criticism examines the marriage between January and May as the kind of economic arrangement that was quite normal in the Middle Ages, but one that devalues the marriage sacrament so that little distinction is made between the values of religion and those of the material world. A relationship between May and Damyan would be impossible to accommodate in such a world.

A Note on Chaucer's English

Chaucer's English has so many similarities with Modern English that it is unnecessary to learn extensive tables of grammar. With a little practice, and using the glosses provided, it should not be too difficult to read the text. Nevertheless, it would be foolish to pretend that there are no differences. The remarks which follow offer some information, hints and principles to assist students who are reading Chaucer's writings for the first time, and to illustrate some of the differences (and some of the similarities) between Middle and Modern English. More comprehensive and systematic treatments of this topic are available in *The Riverside Chaucer* and in D. Burnley, *A Guide to Chaucer's Language*.

1 Inflections

These are changes or additions to words, usually endings, which provide information about number (whether a verb or a noun is singular or plural), tense or gender.

a) Verbs

In the **present** tense most verbs add –e in the first person singular (e.g. *I rede*), –est in the second person singular (*thou biwreyest*), –eth in the third person singular (*he clymbeth*) and –en in the plural. This can be summarized as follows:

	Middle English	Modern English
Singular	1 I telle	I tell
	2 Thou tellest	You tell
	3 He/She/It telleth	He/She/It tells
Plural	1 We tellen	We tell
	2 Ye tellen	You tell
	3 They tellen	They tell

As you can see, Middle English retains more inflections than Modern English, but the system is simple enough. Old English, the phase of the language between around 449 CE, when the Angles first came to Britain, and about 1100, had many more inflections.

In describing the **past** tense it is necessary to begin by making a distinction, which still applies in Modern English, between strong and weak verbs. **Strong verbs** form their past tense by changing their stem (e.g. I sing, I sang; you drink, you drank; he fights, he fought; we throw, we threw), while **weak verbs** add to the stem (I want, I wanted; you laugh, you laughed; he dives, he dived).

In the past tense in Middle English, strong verbs change their stems (e.g. *sing* becomes *sang* or *song*) and add –e in the second person singular (e.g. *thou songe*) and –en in the plural (e.g. *they songen*). Weak verbs add –de or –te (e.g. *fele* becomes *felte*, *here* becomes *herde*) with –st in the second person singular (e.g. *thou herdest*) and –n in the plural (e.g. *they felten*). The table below compares the past tense in Middle and Modern English for strong and weak verbs.

Strong verbs		
	Middle English Present stem: 'sing'	**Modern English**
Singular	1 I sange (or soonge) 2 Thou songe 3 He/She/It sange	I sang (or sung) You sang He/She/It sang
Plural	1 We songen 2 Ye songen 3 They songen	We sang You sang They sang
Weak verbs		
	Middle English Present stem: 'here'	**Modern English**
Singular	1 I herde 2 Thou herdest 3 He/She/It herde	I heard You heard He/She/It heard
Plural	1 We herden 2 Ye herden 3 They herden	We heard You heard They heard

The past tense can also be formed using the auxiliary verb *gan* plus the past participle, e.g. *gan he borwe*: he borrowed (667), *gan pullen*: pulled (1141). Some verbs add initial y to make their past participle, e.g. *yblessed*: blessed (607), *ypassed*: passed (680), *ytake*: taken (1056).

b) Nouns and adjectives

Nouns mostly add –s or –es for plural, e.g. *freendes* (185), but notice the possessive, e.g. *Goddes* (99). There are no apostrophes in Middle English, although modern editors sometime add one to indicate that a letter has been elided, e.g. *th'effect* (186), *th'onour* (237). Some nouns add –en for plural, e.g. *yen, eyen*: eyes (855, 1148). Although (unlike modern French or German) nouns do not take grammatical gender in Middle English, some nouns do add –e for feminine. Some adjectives add –e for the plural, and some are converted to adverbs by the addition of –e, e.g. *faire* (1085).

c) Personal pronouns

The forms of the personal pronouns are somewhat different from those used in Modern English and are worth recording in full:

		Subject	Object	Possessive
Singular	1	I, ich	me	myn, my
	2	Thou, thow	thee	thyn, thy
	3 masculine	He	hym, him	his
	3 feminine	She	her	hir, hire
	3 neuter	It, hit	it, hit	his
Plural	1	We	us	owre, our, owres
	2	Ye	you, yow	your, youres
	3	They	hem	hire, here

Remember that the distinction between *thou* and *you* in Middle English often involves politeness and social relationship as well as number. This is similar to modern French or German. Thus *thou* forms are used with friends, family and social inferiors, *you* forms with strangers or superiors. In *The Merchant's Prologue and Tale* the Host uses the *you* form when talking to the Merchant, and January addresses his bride in this same polite form at first, but later he uses *thou* when speaking to May.

2 Relative pronouns

The main **relative pronouns** found are *that* and *which*. In translating *that* it is often wise to try out a range of Modern English equivalents, such as *who, whom, which*. The prefix *ther–* in such words as *therto* and *therwith* often refers back to the subject matter of the previous phrase. *Therto* may be translated as 'in addition to all that' or 'in order to achieve that'.

3 Impersonal construction

With certain verbs the **impersonal construction** is quite common, e.g. *bifel*: it happened (1013), *hym thoughte*: it seemed to him (394).

4 Reflexive pronouns

Many verbs can be used with a **reflexive pronoun**, a pronoun which refers back to the subject (as in modern French or German) and which may, depending on the verb employed, be translated or understood as part of the verb, e.g. *spede yow* (715), *dispeire yow noght* (457).

5 Extra negatives

In Middle English extra **negatives** often make the negative stronger, whereas in Modern English double negatives cancel each other out, e.g. *ne children sholde I none* (225), *ne to no creature* (844), *ne se ye nat* (1042), *ne be nat wrooth* (1074).

6 Contraction

Sometimes pronouns merge with their associated verbs, e.g. *shaltow*: shall you (274), *hastow*: have you (354), *dostow*: do you (1155).

7 Word order

Middle English **word order** is often freer than Modern English, and in particular there is more inversion of subject and verb (e.g. *Al passed was his siknesse and his sorwe* [798]) or subject and complement (e.g. *To eten hem alle he nas no thyng eschu* [600]). In analysing difficult sentences you should first locate the verb, then its subject, then the object or complement. (Roughly, a verb which involves activity takes an object – she hit the ball, he gave her the book – while a verb which describes a state of affairs takes a complement – it was yellow, you look better.) Then you should put these elements together. It should then be easier to see how the various qualifiers fit in.

Chaucer sometimes adds to his sentences in ways that would not be considered 'good English' today. For example, the sentence beginning in line 595, in which the Merchant describes January's eager preparations for his wedding night when his guests finally leave, consists of so many clauses and phrases that in modern English it would seem a very long, convoluted sentence:

> He drynketh ypocras, clarree, and vernage
> Of spices hoote t'encreessen his corage;
> And many a letuarie hath he ful fyn,
> Swiche as the cursed monk, daun Constantyn,
> Hath writen in his book *De Coitu*;
> To eten hem alle he nas no thyng eschu.
>
> (line 595–600)

Written in modern English this would probably become two or three sentences, but Chaucer achieves his effects by letting the sentence develop out of the long list of aphrodisiacs that January takes in the build-up to the comic climax of his wedding night.

8 Connection of clauses

Middle English often does not indicate **connection of clauses** as clearly as Modern English. In seeking to understand or in translating you may need to provide connecting words. On occasion you may have to provide verbs which have been omitted, particularly the verb 'to be' or verbs of motion. You may also need to regularize number or tense (in some Middle English sentences a subject can shift from singular to plural, or a verb from present to past).

Chaucer can mix the past tense with the historic present (sometimes in telling a story we use the present tense, even though we and our audience know that the events occurred in the past) but a Modern English writer would have to maintain consistency at least within the sentence and usually within the paragraph as well. Chaucer's usage here (and with the implied words and the lack of connectives) may well be closer to spoken English than modern formal writing could be.

9 Change of meaning

Although most of the words which Chaucer uses are still current (often with different spellings) in Modern English, some of them have changed their meaning. So it is a good idea to check the Notes or the Glossary even for the words which look familiar. If you are interested in investigating the ways in which words change their meanings over time, you can look at the quotations provided in large historical dictionaries, such as the *Oxford English Dictionary* or the *Shorter Oxford Dictionary* or in R.W. Burchfield, *The English Language* (Oxford, 1985), pages 113–123, or G. Hughes, *Words in Time: A Social History of English Vocabulary* (Blackwell). Some examples from *The Merchant's Prologue and Tale* are shown in the table below.

Middle English	(line number)	Meaning	Equivalent modern word
assenteden	(358)	agreed	assented
beren	(146)	hold	bear
bit	(165)	instructed	bid

Middle English	(line number)	Meaning	Equivalent modern word
catel	(313)	property, goods	cattle
corage	(42)	desire	courage
condescended	(393)	decided	condescended
delicat	(434)	delightful	delicate
drenche	(989)	drown	drench
desolat	(109)	lonely	desolate
gentil	(783)	noble, virtuous	gentle
knyt	(179)	united	knit
lusty	(183)	happy, pleasant	lusty
sadnesse	(392)	seriousness	sadness
scrit	(485)	document	script
sterve	(80)	die	starve

A Note on Pronunciation

The Merchant's Prologue and Tale, like other poems, benefits from being read aloud. Even if you read it aloud in a Modern English pronunciation you will get more from it, but Middle English was pronounced differently (the sounds of a language change at least as much as the vocabulary or the constructions) and it helps to make some attempt at a Middle English accent. The best way to learn this is to imitate one of the recordings (those issued by Pavilion and Argo are especially recommended for this purpose). A few principles are given below; more can be found in *The Riverside Chaucer*.

1 In most cases you should pronounce all consonants (for example you should sound the 'k' in *knight* and the 'l' in *half*). But in words of French origin initial 'h' (as in *habitacioun*, for example) should not be sounded, nor should 'g' in the combination 'gn'. The combination 'gh', as in *right* (218, 220), is best sounded 'ch' as Scottish 'loch'.

2 In most cases all vowels are sounded, though a final 'e' may be silent because of elision with a vowel following (e.g. do not sound the 'e' in *namoore of* [232]) or because of the stress pattern of the line (e.g. I would not sound the final 'e' in *leeste* [679] and *feeste* [680]).

3 Two points of spelling affect pronunciation. When 'y' appears as a vowel you should sound it as 'i' (see table on page 136). Sometimes a 'u' sound before 'n' or 'm' was written 'o' (because 'u' and 'n' look very similar in the handwriting of the time). This means that *song* and *yong* should be pronounced 'sung' and 'yung'. This also applies in *comen* and *sonne* (as in their Modern English equivalents 'come' and 'son').

4 You will not go too far wrong with combinations of vowels, such as *ai*, *eu* and *oy* if you sound them as in Modern English. There are significant exceptions (for example *hous* [876, 1070] and many words of similar ending should be pronounced with an *oo*

sound) but it is not possible to establish reliable rules purely on the basis of the spelling.

5 The principal vowel sounds differ somewhat from Modern English. They are set out in the table below (adapted from Norman Davis's table in *The Riverside Chaucer*). The table distinguishes long and short versions of each vowel. This distinction still applies in Modern English (consider the 'a' sounds in 'hat' and 'father') but unfortunately it is often only possible to decide whether a particular vowel is long or short by knowing about the derivation of the word. Do not despair. Even a rough approximation will help you. Only experts in medieval languages have reliable Middle English accents, and even they cannot be sure that Chaucer would have approved them.

Vowel	Middle English example	Modern equivalent sound
Long 'a'	name (381), cas (658)	'a' in father
Short 'a'	nat (651), that (673)	'a' in hat
Long 'e'	she (10), been (4)	'a' in fate
Open 'e'	deeth (848), breste (884)	'e' in there
Short 'e'	gentil (990), wende (1181)	'e' in set
Unstressed 'e'	sonne (583)	'a' in about, 'e' in forgotten
Long 'i'	I (2), tyme (592)	'i' in machine
Short 'i'	hym (60), right (220)	'i' in sit
Long 'o'	no (84), moot (616)	'o' in note
Open 'o'	hooly (49)	'oa' in broad
Short 'o'	som (195)	'o' in hot
Long 'u'	hous (876)	'oo' in boot
Short 'u'	but (210), ful (243)	'u' in put

Essay Questions

1 Explore the ways in which Chaucer presents attitudes towards marriage in *The Merchant's Tale*.

2 In what ways is the setting of January's garden important in *The Merchant's Tale*?

3 How far do you think the tale the Merchant tells is in keeping with what you learn about his character?

4 Examine the presentation of January in *The Merchant's Tale*.

5 Remind yourself of lines 55–180 of the tale. How does the Merchant present his views here?

6 One critic has written of *The Merchant's Tale* that it 'transcends the traditional medieval criticism of women for their seductive powers and inconstancy in love; equally important is the tale's demonstration of the reprehensible folly and lechery of men'. How far do agree with this view?

7 Explore the ways in which Chaucer ends *The Merchant's Tale*. In your answer you should examine in detail the passage from line 1142 to the end of the tale.

8 How important is the use of *auctoritees* to the overall effect that Chaucer creates in the tale?

9 How do Pluto and Proserpina make an important contribution to the overall effect of the tale?

10 Examine Chaucer's use of imagery in *The Merchant's Tale*. Write in detail about two or three selected passages in your answer.

11 'The use of symbolism in *The Merchant's Tale* is an important element in the development of Chaucer's effects.' Explore Chaucer's use of symbolism in the tale and evaluate its contribution to the tale overall.

12 How are attitudes towards love and marriage presented in *The Merchant's Tale*?

13 How important is Chaucer's use of irony to the overall effect of *The Merchant's Tale*?

14 *Mayus, that sit with so benyngne a chiere, / Hire to biholde it semed fayerye* (530–531). Examine the presentation of May in *The Merchant's Tale*. You should write in detail about two or three selected passages in your answer.

15 'Damyan is nothing more than the stock seducer of the fabliau.' How far do you agree with this view?

16 What contribution do Placebo and Justinus make to *The Merchant's Tale*?

17 What view of women do you think Chaucer wanted his audience to gain from *The Merchant's Prologue and Tale*?

18 What anti-feminist views does *The Merchant's Prologue and Tale* present, and does it offer any counter views? You should use specific references to the text to support your ideas.

19 Explore the significance of the idea of blindness in *The Merchant's Tale*.

20 Examine the presentation of January's views on marriage in *The Merchant's Tale*. You should write in detail about two or three selected passages, or range more widely in your answer.

Chronology

c. 1340–45 Geoffrey Chaucer born in London to John and Agnes Chaucer.

1357 Chaucer becomes a page in the household of Elizabeth, the Countess of Ulster and Lionel, Earl of Ulster (second son of Edward III).

1359 September: Edward III invades France; Chaucer serves in the army and goes to France in the retinue of Lionel.

1360 Chaucer is captured at Reims and ransomed for £16; carries letters from France to England for Prince Lionel.

c. 1365 Chaucer marries Philippa Roet, who is employed in the Queen's household.

1367 Enters service as a squire in the household of Edward III.

c. 1367–70 Translates *Romaunt of the Rose*.

1369 Chaucer returns to France and serves in the army of John of Gaunt.

c. 1369–70 Writes *The Book of the Duchess* to commemorate the death of Blanche, Duchess of Lancaster.

1372 Chaucer is sent to Italy on a diplomatic mission on behalf of the king.

1374 Edward III appoints Chaucer Controller of the Customs for hides, skins and wool for the port of London.

1376–8 Chaucer makes several journeys to France and Flanders on important diplomatic business.

1378 Travels to Milan on a diplomatic mission.

c. 1378–82 Chaucer writes *The House of Fame* and *The Parliament of Fowls*.

c. 1382–7 Writes *Troilus and Criseyde*, *Palamoun and Arcite* and *The Legend of Good Women*.

1385–6 Appointed Justice of the Peace for Kent.

1386 Elected as a Member of Parliament and retires as Controller of Customs.

1387 Chaucer's wife dies.

1387–92 Begins *The Canterbury Tales*, writing the *General Prologue* and some of the tales.

1389 Appointed Clerk of the King's Works by Richard II.

1391 Retires as Clerk of the King's Works and is appointed Deputy Forester of the Royal Forest of North Petherton in Somerset.

1391–2 Writes *The Treatise of the Astrolabe*.

c. 1392–1400 Writes more of *The Canterbury Tales*.

1400 25 October: Chaucer dies and is buried in Westminster Abbey.

Further Reading

Editions

The following editions have useful notes and glossaries:

Larry D. Benson, *The Riverside Chaucer* (Oxford University Press, 1988)

Maurice Hussey (ed.), *The Merchant's Prologue and Tale* (Cambridge University Press, 1966)

Sheila Innes (ed.), *The Merchant's Prologue and Tale* (Cambridge University Press, 2001)

Background reading on Chaucer and his works

Ian Bishop, *The Narrative Art of the Canterbury Tales* (Everyman's Library, 1988)

Piero Boitani and Jill Mann (eds), *The Cambridge Companion to Chaucer* (Cambridge University Press, 1986)

Muriel Bowden, *A Reader's Guide to Geoffrey Chaucer* (Thames and Hudson, 1964)

Derek Brewer, *An Introduction to Chaucer* (Longman, 1984)

Helen Cooper, *Oxford Guides to Chaucer: The Canterbury Tales* (Oxford University Press, 1989)

S.S. Hussey, *Chaucer: An Introduction* (Methuen, 1981)

G.A. Rudd, *Geoffrey Chaucer* (Routledge, 2001)

Criticism

J.J. Anderson (ed.), *The Canterbury Tales: A Selection of Critical Essays* (Macmillan Casebook Series, 1974)

George Lyman Kittredge, 'Chaucer's Discussion of Marriage' (*Modern Philology* IX, 1911–1912), available at http://sites.fas.harvard.edu/~chaucer/canttales/franklin/marriage.html, also published in Macmillan Casebook Series edition

Stephanie A. Tolliver, January's Misogynist Merchant: The Theme of Sight in Chaucer's Merchant and 'The Merchant's Tale' (The University of Virginia's College at Wise, 2001), available at http://www.luminarium.org/medlit/tolliver.htm This article also contains a useful bibliography

T. Williams, *The Merchant's Prologue and Tale* (York Notes Advanced, Longman, 2003)

Glossary

abregge shorten
adversitee setback, problem
agast afraid
ago gone
al although (1060)
alday always
alderfirst first of all
aleyes garden paths (lit. alleys) (1112)
algate completely
altercacioun argument, difference
apayen satisfy
apoynted decided
arwe arrow
assayen prove, test
assente agree
assoilleth solve, answer
aswage assuage, lessen
at al in every way
attemprely in moderation
auctoritee authority (i.e. supported by classical scholars)
avaunt boast
avoutrye adultery
avysement careful consideration
axen ask

bedeth waits
bely-naked completely naked
bene bean
bene-straw bean straw
benyngnely graciously
benyngnytee graciousness
benyson blessing
berynge bearing
bifel occurred, happened
bille document, letter

bisette employed, used
bit bade, instructed
bityde befall, happen to
biwaille bewail, lament
biwreye reveal
blent blind, deceived
blosme blossom
bond pledge
boond bound, tied
bountee goodness, virtue
bowe bone
bredeth spreads, starts
brenneth burns
brent burnt
brere briar
breste break
brotilnesse fickleness
bryd bird
buxom obedient

catel possessions, property
chaast chaste
charge load
chartres contract
cheere lechery
chees choose
chevyssaunce financial arrangements
chidestere nagging, scolding woman
clapte to shut, closed
clarre sweet wine
clasped fastened
clene morally pure
clerke scholar
clippeth embraces
cloutes pieces (741)

clyket   key
cokewold   cuckold, husband whose wife is unfaithful
coltissh   energetic, frisky (like a colt or young horse)
columbyn   dove
commune   common land
conseil   counsel, advice; secret (1219)
constellacion   constellations (the influence of the stars)
corage   courage; sexual desire (547)
corse   curse
countrefeten   copy, duplicate
coveitise   covetousness, greed (954)
craft   skill; craftiness
craketh   croaks
croucheth hem   blesses them (with the sign of the cross)
curious   careful, painstaking
curteisye   noble behaviour, courtesy

daun   academic title, BA
dawe   dawn; see clearly
debaat   difference of opinions
deceyvable   deceptive
declynacion   declination (astrological term)
deffie   defy
delicat   delicious, delightful
deme   judge
descryve   describe
desolat   lonely
despended   spent
dette   debt
devyse   think about, imagine

deyntee   delight
deys   dais, raised platform
discreet   tactful
dispeire   despair
dispence   expenditure
disport   pleasure
disporten   play
disputisoun   disagreement
diurne   daily
diverse   different
dostow   do you
dote   become senile
doutelees   without a doubt
dowve   dove
drede   fear, doubt
drenche   drown
dressen   prepare, get ready
dronkelewe   heavy drinker, drunkard
dure   last, endure

eek   also
eft   again
eggying   encouragement
elde   old age
elles   otherwise
empeyre   harm, injure
enhaunce   exalt, raise up
enquere   investigate
ensample   example
entende   attend
entente   intention
ententyf   attentive, devoted
envenymynge   poisoning
er   before
eschue   reject, avoid
espye   discover, find out
estatly   dignified
esy   comfortable

everychon everyone
everydeel everything
exaltacion rising (astrological term)
eyle ail, be ill

fader father
famulier familiar; courteous, friendly
fantasye delusion, fancy
fareth goes
fayn glad, eager
feffed endowed
felicitee happiness
fetisly elegantly
fette fetch
feyne pretend
firmament sky
flekked pye magpie
folwe follow
folye foolishness
forage cattle fodder
forbere endure
forgoon forgo, give up
forthynke cause regret
fostre care for, look after
franchise generosity, nobility of spirit
ful very
ful yoore ago a long time ago
fyn fine; end, outcome (894)
fyrbrond fire-brand, torch

gadere gather
gaf gave
game fun
gan did; began
gees geese
gentillesse noble character

gesse believe
glose gloss over
glymsyng impaired vision
governaunce behaviour, self-control, management
grace favour
grisely frightening

habounde abound (i.e. be plentiful)
hals neck
halt considers
hardily assuredly, certainly
hastif hasty
heng hung
heritage property, inheritance
hertely gladly
highte called
hool well, in good health
hoor white haired
houndfyssh dogfish
housbondrye household economy

ilke same
instaunce request
instrumentz musical instruments
inwith in

jalousie jealousy
jangleresse female gossip
jape play a trick
jargon chatter

kan can; know (456)
keep heed
kembe comb
knave servant
knyt united
konne know about

koude   could
kyd   made known
kynde   generous (1177)

labbyng   gossiping
laurer   laurel tree
lay   song, poem
leccherye   lust
lechour   lustful person
leere   learn
leeve   believe
leste   choose, please
lete   hinder, prevent; leave (1005)
letuarie   remedy, medicine
leve   leave, permission
levere   rather
lewed   ignorant; gullible (1063)
leyser   leisure
list   want
liste   like to
lust   pleasure, inclination; wants (132)
lusty   happy, pleasant
lymes   limbs

make   mate
manace   threaten
mannyssh wood   man-mad
mantel   cloak
marchal   master of ceremonies
matiere   matter, business
mayde   maiden, young woman
maystow   may you
maze   be confused, bewildered
meene   instrument, means
mekeste   meekest
meschief   trouble
mete   food
meynee   group, gathering

mo   more
moebles   moveable possessions, personal property
mooder   mother
moot   must
morwe   morning
moste   must
mottelee   cloth made up of various colours
mowe   may
muchel   much
murye   merry
myddel smal   slim waist
mynstralcye   music and singing
myschaunce   bad luck
mysconceyveth   misunderstands
mysdemeth   misjudges
myssayd   misspoken, said something wrong

naddre   adder
namely   especially
namoore   no more
nas   was not
nathelees   nevertheless
ne   not; nor
no fors   no matter
nolde   would not
noot   do not know
nyce   foolish
nys   is not

o   one (123)
observances   duties
offende   do wrong to, injure
ones   once
oon   one
ootherweys   otherwise
orisons   prayers

other mo   many more
overmacche   outdo

paleys   palace
panyer   basket
papejay   parrot
paramour   sexual desire
paraunter   perhaps
paraventure   perhaps; by chance
pardee   by God; indeed
parfit   perfect
parfourned   performed
parte   share; divide
passe   pass; surpass
passyng   extreme
pees   peace
penner   writing case
pere   pear
pestilence   plague
peyne   pain; suffering
peynte   paint; disguise
pilwe   pillow
pitee   pity, compassion
pitte   grave
plesaunce   pleasure, delight
poure   gaze
povre   poor
precious   fastidious, prudish (750)
preve   prove
preyneth   trims
preyse   praise
privee   secret (893)
procreacioun   procreation, reproduction
prudence   good judgement
pryen   peer
pryvee   latrine, lavatory (742)
purpos   intention(s)
purtreyed   imagined

pye   magpie
pyk   pike (large freshwater fish)
pykerel   young pike
pyrie   pear tree

queynte   strange
quod   said

ragerye   passion
rede   counsel, advise
reed   advice
reherce   speak about
rekke   care, pay attention
renne   run
rente   tore
repreve   reproach
rewe   take pity
reynes   rains
route   crowd (338); group, company (347)
routhe   pity
rownynge   whispering
rude   plain; rough
ryve   tear

sad   serious
sadnesse   seriousness, steadfastness
sapience   wisdom
saugh   saw
savacion   salvation
scole-termes   scholarly references
scrit   document
seculeer   secular, not in holy orders
seelde   seldom, rarely
sely   foolish; innocent; simple
semblable   similar; like
sentence   opinion; sense
servysable   of use, of service

shaltow   shall you

shap   figure

shape   prepare; create

sheene   shining, radiant

shent   damned; ruined

shilde   shield, protect

shrewe   nagging and bad-
tempered woman

shynke   pour out

sickerly   certainly

sikernesse   security

sith   since

sleighte   trick

slow   slew, killed

sodeyn hap   sudden chance
happening

solas   comfort

someres   summer

sooth   true

sorwe   sorrow

sotilly   craftily, stealthily

spedde   succeeded

spot   stain; harm

stant   stood

stapen   advanced

stark   strong

stedefast   faithful

sterve   die

stirte   rushed, went quickly

stoore   bold, crude

strepe   strip

streyne   force

studieth   thought carefully

subtil   subtle, discreet

suffisant   adequate, suitable

suffre   endure, allow

swynke   work

swyve   have sex with

syk   ill

syke   sigh

t'espien   to see, to find out

take no kep   take no notice

tarye   delay

terrestre   earthly

thenk   consider

thewes   personal qualities

thilke   that

throng   thrust

travers   curtain

trespacen   do wrong

tretee   agreement

tromped   sounded a trumpet

trowe   believe

tweye   two

twiste   branch

unbounden   free (i.e. unmarried)

unlikly   not pleasing

unshette   unlocked

unstable   changeable

usage   custom

vanytee   illusion

venym   poison

vernage   strong sweet wine

verraily   certainly; truly; fully

vitaille   food

voyde   empty

wan   won

wastour   extravagant person (i.e.
waster of money)

wele   happiness

wenche   common woman

wene   believe

wex   wax

weyve   turn away, deviate from

whilom   once
wight   person
wirche   work; act
wit   knowledge; sense
wite   know; find out
wood   mad
woot   know
woxen   become
wrooth   angry
wydwe   widow
wyflees   wifeless
wyket   gate
wyse   way, manner (373, 555)

yaf   gave
ybroght   brought
ycoupled   married
ydolastre   idol worshipper
yelde   yield, give up
yen   eyes
yeve   give
yifte   gift
ynogh   enough
yok   yoke, harness
yore   a long time ago
ypocras   hippocras (spiced drink)
ysatled   settled down
yse   see
Ytaille   Italy
yvele   evil
ywoxen   grown
ywroght   made